Inhaltsübersicht

Etwa die Hälfte der Tonaufnahmen zu diesem Heft wurde nach einer ausformulierten Textvorlage aufgenommen. Diese finden Sie als kostenloses Online-Angebot auf unserer Website **www.englishg.de** unter >Downloads<.

Die andere Hälfte wurde frei gesprochen, d. h. ohne ausformulierte Textvorlage aufgenommen, und liegt deshalb nicht in schriftlicher Form vor.

VORWORT

Die Vorschläge zur Leistungsmessung

Im Mittelpunkt der Unterrichtsentwicklung steht seit geraumer Zeit die Kompetenzorientierung. Die Schülerinnen und Schüler sollen nicht mehr in erster Linie gelerntes Wissen wiedergeben, sondern sie sollen zeigen, in welchem Maße sie bereits kommunikative, aber auch methodische, soziale und personale Kompetenzen beherrschen. Im Unterricht stehen die selbstständige Aneignung von Wissen und Strategien sowie die Bereitschaft und Fähigkeit zu lebenslangem Lernen im Vordergrund. Die Schüler/innen gestalten ihre Lern- und Arbeitsprozesse auf altersgemäße Weise mit und arbeiten mit anderen zusammen. Vor diesem Hintergrund spielen die Leistungsmessung und Leistungsbeurteilung eine besondere Rolle, weil sie den Lernenden eine Rückmeldung über den erreichten Lernstand geben. Während der Unterricht darauf abzielt, Kompetenzen zu erwerben, zu vertiefen und immer weiter auszudifferenzieren, soll die Lernerfolgsmessung Gelegenheit bieten, das Gelernte unter Beweis zu stellen. Klassenarbeiten sollten nach Möglichkeit eine Zusammenstellung mehrerer Teilaufgaben sein, die rezeptive und produktive Leistungen überprüfen.

Die einzelnen Aufgaben der **Vorschläge zur Leistungsmessung** sind so gestaltet, dass sie einerseits auf die sprachlichen und thematischen Bereiche der jeweiligen Unit eingehen, aber darüber hinaus auch die persönlichen Vorstellungen und Erfahrungen der Lernenden abrufen. Sie sind alters- und situationsgerecht gestaltet. Zur Bewältigung der Aufgaben erhalten die Schülerinnen und Schüler eindeutige Arbeitsanweisungen, so dass sie von Anfang an genau wissen, worauf es bei der Lösung der jeweiligen Aufgaben ankommt. Die Abfolge der Aufgaben für die einzelnen Units orientiert sich in der Regel an den Kategorien der Bildungsstandards und Lehrpläne:

Kommunikative Kompetenzen
- Hörverstehen
- Sprechen
- Leseverstehen
- Schreiben
- Sprachmittlung

Verfügbarkeit sprachlicher Mittel
- Wortschatz
- Grammatik

Wie in den früheren Bänden der **Vorschläge zur Leistungsmessung** gibt es zu jeder Unit des Schülerbuches ein Angebot an Aufgaben für Tests und Klassenarbeiten. Darüber hinaus enthält dieser Band zwei weitere Aufgabensammlungen: Das ***Exam File*** bietet prüfungsrelevante Aufgaben zur Überprüfung aller Kompetenzen; das Kapitel ***Oral Exams*** enthält zwanzig Aufgaben zur Überprüfungen der mündlichen Kompetenz der Schülerinnen und Schüler – zehn für Einzelprüfungen und zehn für Tandemprüfungen.
Die Aufgaben und Übungen, die zu jeder Unit zur Verfügung stehen, stellen ein Angebot dar, aus dem von Fall zu Fall ausgewählt werden kann oder auch ausgewählt werden muss, wenn beispielsweise bestimmte Aufgabenformate nicht in Klassenarbeiten verwendet werden sollen. Den Schwerpunkt bei der Zusammenstellung von Klassenarbeiten sollten kompetenzorientierte Aufgaben bilden.
Es gibt zu jeder Unit zwei Aufgaben zum Hörverstehen. Es können längere Hörtexte, in denen ein bestimmtes Thema zusammenhängend dargeboten wird, ebenso ausgewählt werden wie solche, die aus mehreren kurzen Hörpassagen bestehen, z. B. Telefonauskünften, Mitteilungen, oder Kurzinformationen. Etwa die Hälfte der Texte wurde frei gesprochen, d. h. ohne ausformulierte Textvorlagen aufgenommen.
Zur Überprüfung des Leseverstehens werden pro Unit zwei bis drei unterschiedliche Texte angeboten. Mit Blick auf die Abschlussprüfungen am Ende der Klasse 10 sollten Klassenarbeiten auf die relevanten Prüfungsformate vorbereiten. Das ist bei allen Aufgaben und Aufgabentypen von Anfang an bedacht worden.

Um eine einzelne Kompetenz, bestimmte sprachliche Mittel oder eine bestimmte Lerntechnik zu überprüfen, kommen geschlossene Aufgabenformate zum Tragen:
- Zuordnungsaufgaben
- Selektionsaufgaben
- Transformationsaufgaben
- Lückenaufgaben

Stärker sprachproduktive Aufgaben verlangen von den Schülerinnen und Schülern
- das Beantworten von Fragen zu einem Text
- die Vervollständigung von Tabellen etc.

Offene Aufgabenformate steuern die Lösungsaktivität nur in sehr geringem Maße:
- Berichte über bestimmte Geschehnisse
- Briefe, E-Mails

Ein Grundprinzip bei der Gestaltung der kompetenzorientierten Aufgaben besteht darin, dass jeweils die Kompetenz überprüft wird, die im Mittelpunkt der jeweiligen Aufgabe steht – und möglichst nur die. Wenn es um die Überprüfung der Lesekompetenz geht, werden Aufgabentypen angeboten, die diese Fertigkeit möglichst exakt und objektiv erfassen. Dazu gehören *multiple choice questions, multiple matching exercises, short open answer questions, table completion, true / false / not given exercises.*

Wenn bei der Überprüfung der Lese- bzw. Hörverstehenskompetenz *write in*-Aufgaben bearbeitet werden, sollte beachtet werden, dass sprachliche Verstöße nicht zu einem Punktabzug führen, da die Kompetenz *Writing* hier nicht getestet wird. Dies erfolgt in einigen Units durch Schreibaufgaben, die im Anschluss an Lesetexte eingesetzt werden können.

Zu den Vorschlägen zur Leistungsmessung in diesem Heft gehören selbstverständlich auch Aufgaben zur Grammatik und Lexik, da die Beherrschung sprachlicher Mittel untrennbar zum Fremdsprachenerwerb gehört. Hier muss – je nach bundeslandspezifischen Anforderungen – ausgewählt werden.

In einigen Bundesländern wird in jüngster Zeit empfohlen, mindestens eine Klassenarbeit herkömmlicher Art pro Schuljahr durch eine andere gleichwertige Form zu ersetzen: Im Englischunterricht sollen in einer mündlichen Klassenarbeit die dialogische und monologische Sprechkompetenz überprüft werden. Die in diesem Heft angebotenen Aufgaben – sowohl in den drei Units als auch in den Kapiteln ***Exam File*** und ***Oral Exams*** – können für diese Form der alternativen Leistungsüberprüfungen verwendet werden. Den Schülerinnen und Schülern sollte dabei eine angemessene Vorbereitungszeit eingeräumt werden. Die tabellarische Übersicht auf S. 4 stellt mögliche Bewertungskriterien dar.

Im Rahmen von Klassenarbeiten spielen grundsätzlich geschlossene, halboffene und offene Aufgabenformate zusammen. Rezeptive Kompetenzen wie das Seh-/Hörverstehen und das Lesen werden im Wesentlichen in Form von geschlossenen und halboffenen Aufgaben überprüft. Im Sinne einer integrativen Überprüfung aller Kompetenzen sollten Klassenarbeiten nach Möglichkeit eine Mischung verschiedener Aufgabenformen umfassen.

Beurteilungskriterien

Es ist von besonderer Bedeutung, Leistungsfeststellungen und vor allem Klassenarbeiten so anzulegen, dass die Notengebung für die Schüler/innen transparent ist und die jeweilige Überprüfung hinreichend Erkenntnisse über die individuelle Lernentwicklung liefert. Eine kriteriengeleitete Bewertung ist einer fehlerorientierten, die z. B. von einem Fehlerquotienten ausgeht, vorzuziehen. Häufig wird zwischen einer inhaltlichen und einer sprachlichen Aufgabenbewältigung unterschieden, wobei die Gewichtung dieser beiden Bereiche von Bundesland zu Bundesland verschieden ist. Das bedeutet, dass die Vorschläge zur Bewertung individueller Schülerleistungen in diesem Heft den länderspezifischen Bestimmungen oder Fachkonferenzbeschlüssen angepasst werden müssen.

Bei der Bewertung offener Aufgaben, besonders im Bereich des Schreibens, sollten von vornherein klare und für die Schüler/innen nachvollziehbare Kriterien festgelegt werden. Sie können sich beziehen auf:

- inhaltliche Aspekte
- Genauigkeit der Kenntnisse
- Verständlichkeit der Aussagen
- sprachliche Klarheit
- gedankliche Stringenz und inhaltliche Strukturiertheit
- Reichhaltigkeit und Differenziertheit des thematischen und funktionalen Wortschatzes
- Komplexität und Variation des Satzbaus
- grammatische Korrektheit
- orthografische, lexikalische Fehler
- Verstöße gegen Sprachrichtigkeit unter Berücksichtigung einer möglichen Beeinträchtigung der Kommunikation

Die tabellarische Übersicht auf S. 5 stellt mögliche Kriterien dar, mit denen offene Aufgaben zur Überprüfung der Schreibkompetenz nachvollziehbar bewertet werden können. Die Bewertungseinheiten sind selbstverständlich Vorschläge, die individuell angepasst werden müssen, ebenso die Umsetzung in Noten. Diese muss den jeweiligen Bedingungen und rechtlichen Bestimmungen für Klassenarbeiten und Lernkontrollen entsprechen.

Zur leichteren Orientierung bei der Zusammenstellung einer Klassenarbeit oder Lernkontrolle sind in einer einleitenden tabellarischen Übersicht vor jeder Unit angegeben:

- die Seitenzahlen,
- die Titel der Aufgaben,
- Kurzbeschreibungen der Aufgaben,
- die jeweils vorherrschende Kompetenz sowie
- Vorschläge zur Bepunktung der Aufgaben

Bewertungskriterien zur Überprüfung der Grundfertigkeit „Sprechen“ in Klasse 10

	Kommunikative Leistung			Inhaltliche Leistung	Sprachliche Leistung		
Punkte	**Monologisches Sprechen**	**Dialogisches Sprechen**	**Redefluss**	**Inhalt**	**Sprachliche Vielfalt (Lexik und Grammatik)**	**Sprachliche Richtigkeit (Lexik und Grammatik)**	**Aussprache und Intonation**
6	Kommunikative Absicht ist erfüllt; Einzelne Elemente sind verknüpft, ein linearer Aufbau ist erkennbar; Reagiert spontan auf Rückfragen; Zeigt sich – im Rahmen seiner sprachlichen Möglichkeiten – teilweise flexibel	Kann ein Gespräch beginnen, in Gang halten und beenden; Reagiert – teilweise spontan – auf den Gesprächspartner; Zeigt sich – im Rahmen seiner sprachlichen Möglichkeiten – in der Interaktion flexibel	Ist bemüht, flüssig zu sprechen; Wendet vereinzelt Gesprächsstrategien wie Rückfragen und Umschreibungen an	Inhaltliche Anforderungen sind voll erfüllt	Verfügt über die in der Aufgabe geforderte Bandbreite an Lexik und Grammatik, die sprachlichen Mittel sind jedoch begrenzt; Verknüpfungen auch mit „because“	Verstöße gegen sprachliche Korrektheit treten auf, vereinzelt auch systematische Fehler, Verständlichkeit ist aber nicht beeinträchtigt; Weitestgehende Vermeidung von Germanismen	Verständliche Aussprache; Aussprache und Intonation führen nicht zu Missverständnissen
4	Kommunikative Absicht kann erschlossen werden; Isolierte Elemente sind teilweise zwar verknüpft, der Aufbau ist jedoch nicht immer schlüssig; Kann teilweise spontan auf Rückfragen reagieren	Kann ein Gespräch beginnen und beenden; Kann Fragen stellen und auf Fragen reagieren; Rollenidentifikation vorhanden	Redefluss ist stockend; Braucht längere Bedenkzeit	Inhaltliche Anforderungen sind größtenteils erfüllt	Verfügt über elementare sprachliche Muster: Wortgruppen und sehr kurze Sätze; Verknüpfungen wie z. B. „and“, „or“, „but“, „then“	Verstöße gegen sprachliche Normen und systematische Fehler treten auf; Gelegentliche Germanismen; Die Verständlichkeit ist teilweise beeinträchtigt	Größtenteils verständliche Aussprache; Aussprache und Intonation führen vereinzelt zu Missverständnissen
2	Kommunikative Absicht ist unter Anstrengung erschließbar; Isolierte Wendungen werden teilweise verknüpft, dies erzeugt jedoch nur sehr beschränkte Linearität; Reagiert nur verzögert auf Rückfragen	Übernimmt im Gespräch eine passive Rolle; Ist davon abhängig, dass der Gesprächspartner sehr langsam spricht; Benötigt Hilfen wie Wiederholungen und Umschreibungen	Spricht wenig und sehr stockend; Braucht viel Bedenkzeit	Inhaltliche Anforderungen sind nur teilweise erfüllt	Lexik deutlich eingeschränkt und häufige Wiederholungen; Verfügt nur über sehr elementare sprachliche Muster und memorierte Wendungen; Verknüpfungen sind vorhanden, überwiegend mit demselben Konnektor	Verstöße gegen sprachliche Korrektheit und systematische Fehler treten gehäuft auf; Germanismen treten auf; Verständlichkeit ist beeinträchtigt	Aussprache teilweise unverständlich; Aussprache und Intonation führen zu Missverständnissen
0	Kommunikative Absicht ist nicht erkennbar; Keine Reaktion auf Rückfragen	Kann nicht am Gespräch teilnehmen; Reagiert nicht auf den Gesprächspartner	Spricht nicht	Inhaltliche Anforderungen sind nicht erkennbar	Lexik nicht vorhanden; Verfügt über keine sprachlichen Muster	Keine Verständigung möglich	Unverständliche Aussprache

Bewertungskriterien zur Überprüfung der Grundfertigkeit „Schreiben" in Klasse 10

	5 Punkte	4 Punkte	3 Punkte	2 Punkte	1 Punkt	0 Punkte
Textaufbau (Textsortenspezifisch/ Adressatenorientiert)	Der Gedankengang ist klar, der Text ist gegliedert und liest sich flüssig, textsortenspezifische Merkmale wurden beachtet	Der Gedankengang ist klar und meist schlüssig	Der Gedankengang ist insgesamt klar, einzelne Textstellen lesen sich nicht flüssig	Der Gedankengang ist insgesamt noch klar, obwohl sich einige Textstellen nicht flüssig lesen lassen	Der Gedankengang ist an mehreren Stellen nicht klar, mehrere Textstellen lesen sich nicht flüssig	Der Gedankengang ist kaum nachvollziehbar. Der überwiegende Teil des Textes liest sich nicht flüssig
Inhalt	Aufgabenstellung beachtet; Inhaltlich richtig, vollständig und aussagekräftig, originell und kreativ	Aufgabenstellung beachtet; Inhaltlich im Wesentlichen richtig, im Wesentlichen vollständig und aussagekräftig	Aufgabenstellung im Wesentlichen beachtet; Inhaltlich überwiegend richtig	Aufgabenstellung teilweise beachtet; Inhaltlich teilweise lückenhaft, wenig aussagekräftig	Aufgabenstellung nur in Ansätzen beachtet; Inhaltlich lückenhaft, wenig aussagekräftig	Aufgabenstellung kaum beachtet; Inhaltlich bruchstückhaft/falsch, nicht aussagekräftig
Verfügbarkeit sprachlicher Mittel	Lernstufenangemessener Wortschatz und Strukturen, die situationsbezogen und differenziert verwendet werden, um das Thema/die Aufgabe zu bearbeiten; Risikobereitschaft, komplexere Strukturen zu benutzen	Wortschatz und Strukturen reichen aus, um das Thema/ die Aufgabe zu bearbeiten	Wortschatz und Strukturen reichen weitgehend aus, um das Thema/die Aufgabe zu bearbeiten	Wortschatz und Strukturen reichen an einigen Stellen nicht aus, um die Aufgabe zu bearbeiten	Wortschatz und Strukturen sind sehr begrenzt und reichen an mehreren Stellen nicht aus, um das Thema zu bearbeiten	Wortschatz und Strukturen sind so begrenzt, dass sie nicht ausreichen, um das Thema/die Aufgabe zu bearbeiten
Korrektheit	Im Verhältnis zur Textlänge vereinzelte orthografische und/oder grammatische Fehler, die die Verständlichkeit nicht beeinträchtigen	Mehrere geringfügige orthografische und/oder grammatische Fehler, die die Verständlichkeit nicht wesentlich beeinflussen	Eine Vielzahl an geringfügigen und vereinzelt grobe orthografische und/oder grammatische Fehler, die die Verständlichkeit teilweise beeinflussen; Einfache Strukturen werden überwiegend korrekt verwendet, die Verständlichkeit wird nicht beeinträchtigt; Komplexere Strukturen können gelegentlich Fehler aufweisen, die Verständlichkeit kann beeinträchtigt sein	Gehäufte grobe grammatische/orthografische Fehler, die die Verständlichkeit stark beeinflussen	Gehäufte gravierende Fehler, die die Verständlichkeit stark einschränken; Einige einfache Strukturen werden korrekt verwendet, es treten viele elementare Fehler auf, es ist teilweise unklar, was ausgedrückt werden soll	Der Text ist so fehlerhaft, dass er kaum verstanden werden kann

Unit 1 Love life!

Übersicht der Aufgaben

Seite	Aufgabe	Kurzbeschreibung	Kompetenz	Punkte
s	1 **Small talk** **Text 1: At Jo's party** **Text 2: On a train in Britain** **Text 3: At the airport**	Informationen erfassen und *a)* *Multiple-Choice*-Aufgaben lösen *b)* Fragen kurz beantworten *c)* Fragen kurz beantworten	Hörverstehen [1]	 3 7 10
10	2 **My favourite films**	Detailinformationen erfassen und Fragen kurz beantworten	Hörverstehen II	14
11	3 **Depressed**	Mit Hilfe eines Bildes und Impulsen über problematische Situationen sprechen	Monologisches Sprechen[2]	20
12	4 **In the school canteen**	Mit Hilfe von Rollenkarten und Impulsen einen Dialog zwischen einem deutschen Schüler und einem Austauschschüler gestalten	Dialogisches Sprechen	20
13–15	5 **A famous director and a famous film** **Text 1: Sir Ridley Scott** **Text 2: Robin Hood**	Eine Kurzbiographie lesen und sechs Fragen kurz beantworten Eine kurze Kritik lesen und Aussagen als *True/False/Not given* ankreuzen	Leseverstehen I	 6 8
16/17	6 **Tears of a clown**	Einen Textausschnitt aus *The Absolutely True Diary of a Part-Time Indian* von Sherman Alexie lesen und *a)* Kurzbeschreibungen drei Charakteren zuordnen *b)* Adjektive aus einer Liste den Charakteren zuordnen *c)* Zitate aus dem Text der richtigen Person zuordnen und die Bedeutung kurz erläutern	Leseverstehen II	 3 6 12

[1] Die Hörtexte zu dieser Unit wurden frei gesprochen anhand einer vorgegebenen Situation, d. h. ohne ausformulierte Textvorlage aufgenommen. Sie liegen deshalb nicht in schriftlicher Form vor.

[2] Diese Fotos in Farbe finden Sie als kostenloses Online-Angebot auf unserer Website **www.englishg.de** unter >Downloads<.

Seite	Aufgabe	Kurzbeschreibung	Kompetenz	Punkte
18	7 **What should a real friend be like?**	Mit Hilfe von Impulsen einen Text über den „perfekten Freund / die perfekte Freundin“ schreiben	Schreiben I (geeignet auch im Zusammenhang mit Aufgabe 6)	20
18	8 **Lots of problems**	Auf eine von vier angedeuteten E-Mails, in denen Probleme geschildert werden, antworten	Schreiben II	20
18	9 **A film I've watched**	Mit Hilfe von Impulsen über einen kürzlich gesehenen Film schreiben	Schreiben III	20
19	10 **What is this film about?**	Anhand einer deutschen Filmkritik zu *Renn, wenn du kannst* einem englischen Freund den Film beschreiben	Sprachmittlung I	15
19	11 **I've got mail**	Eine E-Mail eines amerikanischen Freundes dem Vater auf Deutsch wiedergeben	Sprachmittlung II	10
20	12 **What a person can be or look like**	*a)* Gegensätzliche Adjektive finden *b)* Synonyme Adjektive finden *c)* Unter Verwendung einiger dieser Adjektive eine Person kurz beschreiben	Wortschatz I	6 3 10
20	13 **Choose the right verb**	Das Verb finden, das in den Satz passt *(Multiple Choice)*	Wortschatz II	4
21	14 **Find the right words**	*a)* Wörter zu Worterklärungen finden *b)* vier Wörter erklären *c)* je vier geeignete Verben zu zwei Substantiven finden	Wortschatz III	6 8 8
22	15 **Family photo**	*a)* Anhand von Fragen ein Foto beschreiben *(present progressive)* *b)* Anhand von Satzfragmenten die Abendgestaltung zweier Personen beschreiben *(simple present)* *c)* Über die eigene Abendgestaltung schreiben	Grammatik	6 6 8

1 LISTENING Small talk 1, 2, 3

a) Text 1: At Jo's party 1

Read the task. Then listen to Nora and Steve chatting at a party. Do the following multiple choice tasks. Tick the correct answer. There's only one correct solution. You will hear the recording once. ____/ 3

1 Nora	*a)* is on holiday in Great Britain for a couple of weeks.	
	b) is visiting her penfriend Jo for a couple of weeks.	
	c) is a student at Jo's school for a couple of weeks.	
	d) is a student at Steve's school for a couple of weeks.	
2 Nora is at Jo's party	*a)* because Jo is her exchange partner.	
	b) because there are lots of exchange students.	
	c) because she wants to meet Steve there.	
	d) because she wants to have some drinks there.	
3 Steve is at Jo's party	*a)* because Jo is his best friend at school.	
	b) because he wants to talk to Nora.	
	c) because he wants to have some fun.	
	d) because he wants to meet Jo.	

b) Text 2: On a train in Britain 2

Listen to two train passengers chatting. Answer the questions with a few words or numbers only. You will hear the recording twice. ____/ 7

1 Where is the man going? ____________________

2 Why has the man come to Britain? ____________________

3 Where is the man from? ____________________

4 Where does the woman live? ____________________

5 What **three** activities does she recommend? ____________________

____

____

c) *Text 3: At the airport* 3

In the following recording you will first hear an announcement and then two people talking to each other.

Read the tasks below. You will hear the recording twice.

Part 1

Listen to the announcement at the airport. Complete the notes in a few words or numbers. ____/ 3

1 flight no. AT254 departing from: London

arriving in: ____________________

2 reason for delay: ____________________

3 new departure time: ____________________

Part 2

Listen to two passengers waiting for their delayed flight. Answer the questions in a few words or numbers. ____/ 7

1 The German passenger is telling the woman something about his trip to Scotland.

a) How long will he be staying there? ____________________

b) What will he be doing in Scotland? (Name **two** things.) ____________________

____

____

2 What does the woman tell him about the island of Mull? (Name **three** facts.) ____________________

____

____

3 What does the woman suggest doing while they are waiting for the flight? ____________________

____

2 LISTENING My favourite films 🎧 4

Read the task. Then listen to Richard who is talking about his film interests. Answer the questions in a few words or numbers only. You will hear the recording twice. ______/ 14

1 What kinds of films does Richard love? (Name **three**.) ______________________

____

2 Which kind of film is more for girls? ______________________

3 Why is *Avatar* his favourite film? (Give **three** reasons.) ______________________

____

____

4 **a)** How often does Richard usually go to the cinema? ______________________

b) What does he like about the cinema? (Give **two** reasons.) ______________________

____

____

5 What does he say about the last DVD he bought? (Name **two** facts.) ______________________

____

6 What is Richard's opinion of film reviews? ______________________

____

7 Richard is planning to go to the cinema at the weekend.

a) When? ______________________

b) What film? ______________________

c) Who with? ______________________

3 SPEAKING Depressed

_____/ 20

What does the photo show? Describe it.
How do you think the person in the photo is feeling?
What might have happened?

Think of a situation when you or a friend were very disappointed and sad.
Talk about this situation.
What did you or your friend do to deal with the problems?
Talk for about ten minutes. You've got ten minutes to prepare your talk.

What does the photo show? Describe it.
How do you think the person in the photo is feeling?
What might have happened?

Think of a situation when you or a friend were very disappointed and sad.
Talk about this situation.
What did you or your friend do to deal with the problems?
Talk for about ten minutes. You've got ten minutes to prepare your talk.

4 SPEAKING In the school canteen

_____/ 20

Partner A

Imagine there's an English exchange student at your school. You meet him or her in the school canteen for the first time. He or she takes a seat at your table.

Start the conversation:

- Introduce yourself and talk to the exchange student.
- Remember how to keep a conversation going.
- Finish the conversation in a friendly way.
- Your dialogue should last for about ten minutes.

Here are some ideas, but you can use other ideas too:

– the food in the canteen

– food you like / don't like

– his/her first impressions of your school

– your school day

– free-time activities

– …?

Partner B

Imagine you are an English exchange student at a German school. You're in the school canteen for lunch. You take a seat at a table with a German student.

He or she starts talking to you. Introduce yourself and answer his/her questions. Ask questions.

- Remember how to keep a conversation going.
- Finish the conversation in a friendly way.
- Your dialogue should last for about ten minutes.

Here are some ideas, but you can use other ideas too:

– the food in the canteen

– food you like / don't like

– your first impressions of the German school

– a school day at the German school

– your school and your school day (differences/similarities)

– free-time activities

– …?

5 READING A famous film director and a famous film

Text 1: Sir Ridley Scott

The film director Ridley Scott was born in 1937 in the North of England. Even as a child he loved films and would sometimes watch the same film time and again at the cinema. He didn't enjoy school except for art lessons, so he went to study at the Royal College of Art in London.

In 1963 Scott began work at the BBC, first as a set designer then as a director. In 1968 he left the BBC and started his own company making adverts. Scott used the money he made from advertising (by 1977 he had made 2,500 TV adverts!) to start making films.

In 1977 Ridley Scott directed *The Duellists*, a historical drama set during the time of Napoleon. The film wasn't very successful in the cinemas, but it won the Jury Prize for Best First Feature at the Cannes Film Festival.

Although Scott was disappointed that *The Duellists* didn't attract more viewers, he kept on making films and his next one, *Alien* (1979), was a hit and became a science fiction classic.

Following *Alien*, the film *Blade Runner* became one of the most important and popular science fiction films of all time. The film (which stars Harrison Ford) was first released in 1982, but had to be changed because of bad reviews. Since then Ridley Scott has released two further versions of the film in 1992 and 2007.

In the years which followed Scott tried to move away from science fiction films, but it wasn't until 1991 that he had a really big success with the film *Thelma and Louise*. The film is a drama about two women's dramatic escape from their everyday lives. It was nominated for six Oscars.

Ridley Scott's next big film was the epic *Gladiator*, starring Russell Crowe. *Gladiator* is a historical film set in Roman times. It was one of the most successful films of the year 2000 and won five Oscars. In 2001 the film *Black Hawk Dawn* showed that Ridley Scott really was one of Hollywood's best directors – the film won two Oscars.

Following *Gladiator*, Ridley Scott has worked with Russell Crowe on other films, including *Body of Lies* (2008) and most recently *Robin Hood* (2010), which you can read more about in the film review.

Read the text and answer the questions in 1–5 words or numbers. _____/ 6

1 Why did Ridley Scott go to study at the Royal College of Art? ______________________

____

2 How many TV adverts did he make between 1968 and 1977? ______________________

3 What was the first film he directed? ______________________

4 Which film had to be changed before it became a famous science fiction film? ______________________

____

5 Which of Ridley Scott's films won five Oscars? ______________________

6 Which actor plays a main role in three of Ridley Scott's films? ______________________

Text 2: Robin Hood

Robin Hood – Film review

The plot

The film is set in 13th century England. Robin is returning from war with his King, Richard the Lionheart. The king dies and Robin and his closest friends decide to return to England to live as free men. But things don't go quite as they planned, and they are followed to Nottingham by the bad guy Sir Godfrey. Sir Godfrey plans to give England to the French and he thinks Robin knows too much about his plans. Robin hopes that the beautiful Marion will marry him. Her home and village are in danger. Robin and his men fight to protect the ones they love and to save their country from war.

The actors

The film stars some very famous actors – Oscar winners Russell Crowe and Cate Blanchett play the lead characters Robin Hood and Maid Marion. Mark Strong (who you may recognize from the film 'Sherlock Holmes') plays Sir Godfrey. He has to fight Robin on more than one occasion!

Best bits

Some of the scenes are very impressive and the sets[1] are very realistic.
The battle[2] with the French Army on the south coast is very exciting, and there are lots of mini-battles throughout the film. The plot is fast moving and the film has a good mix of action and drama. And what do you think of Crowe's Nottingham accent? Any good? He is Australian after all!

Favourite characters

Robin Hood, obviously, and Friar Tuck, played by Mark Addy, is very funny!

Any weak bits?

Definitely not, although some of the scenes are violent, so it's obviously not a film for really young viewers.

Hit or miss?

It's definitely a hit if you like this sort of thing!

---

[1] set *Filmkulisse, Bauten*
[2] battle *Kampf, Schlacht*

Read the text. Then decide if the statements are true, false or not given. Tick the correct box.

_____ / 8

	True	*False*	*Not given*
1 After Robin comes back from war, he plans to fight for England against France.			
2 Robin has to fight to get the woman he loves.			
3 Robin helps to protect his country.			
4 The battle between the French and English army is especially violent.			
5 The film is dramatic and full of action.			
6 People who like comedies should watch *Robin Hood.*			
7 Crowe's normal accent is typical for the Nottingham region.			
8 The film is not suitable for children and viewers with weak nerves.			

6 READING Tears of a clown

This is an extract from "The Absolutely True Diary of a Part-Time Indian" by Sherman Alexie. In this extract Arnold remembers telling Rowdy, his best friend on the reservation, about a girl he loved when they were both 12 years old.

When I was twelve, I fell in love with an Indian girl named Dawn. She was tall and brown and was the best traditional powwow dancer on the rez. Her braids, wrapped in otter fur, were legendary. Of course, she didn't care about me. She mostly made fun of me (she called me Junior High Honky for some reason I never understood). But that just made me love her even more. She was out of my league, and even though I was only twelve, I knew that I'd be one of those guys who always fell in love with the unreachable, ungettable, and uninterested.

One night, at about two in the morning, when Rowdy slept over at my house, I made a full confession.

"Man," I said. "I love Dawn so much."

He was pretending to be asleep on the floor of my room.

"Rowdy," I said. "Are you awake?"

"No."

"Did you hear what I said?"

"No."

"I said I love Dawn so much."

He was quiet.

"Aren't you going to say anything?" I asked.

"About what?"

"About what I just said."

"I didn't hear you say anything."

He was just screwing with me.

"Come on, Rowdy, I'm trying to tell you something major."

"You're just being stupid," he said.

"What's so stupid about it?"

"Dawn doesn't give a shit about you," he said.

And that made me cry. Man, I've always cried easily. I cry when I'm happy or sad. I cry when I'm angry. I cry because I'm crying. It's weak. It's the opposite of warrior.

"Quit crying," Rowdy said.

"I can't help it," I said. "I love her more than I've ever loved anybody."

Yeah, I was quite the dramatic twelve-year-old.

"Please," Rowdy said. "Stop that bawling, okay?"

"Okay, okay," I said. "I'm sorry."

I wiped my face with one of my pillows and threw it across the room.

"Jesus, you're a wimp," Rowdy said.

"Just don't tell anybody I cried about Dawn," I said.

a) *Read the text. Then decide which description is the most suitable for each character. Write the correct letter into the box next to the name. There are two more descriptions than you need.* ____/ 3

Arnold ☐ Dawn ☐ Rowdy ☐

A This person lives on an Indian reservation, is really beautiful and knows it. He/She is cool and not interested in other people's feelings.

B This person lives on an Indian reservation, is really beautiful and knows it. He/She is very funny and makes other people laugh.

C This person lives on an Indian reservation and is a real friend. He/She wants to help a friend and listens carefully to the friend's problems. He/She comforts his/her really unhappy friend.

D This person lives on an Indian reservation and can be quite rude. He/She doesn't seem to listen carefully when a friend speaks to him/her, but he/she still tells this friend the truth.

E This person lives on an Indian reservation, is lovesick and knows it. He/She wants to talk to someone about his/her loved one.

b) *Read the text and match the most suitable adjectives to the characters. There are two words for each character and two that don't match.* ____/ 6

beautiful • cool • lazy • lovesick • rude • thin • tough • unhappy

Arnold: ____________________

Dawn: ____________________

Rowdy: ____________________

c) *Read the text again. Who says these sentences? What do they mean? Write one sentence for each statement.* ____/ 12

	Who says it?	**What do they mean?**
1 She was out of my league. (l. 4)		
2 He was just screwing with me. (l. 20)		
3 I'm trying to tell you something major. (l. 21)		
4 Dawn doesn't give a shit about you. (l. 24)		
5 It's the opposite of warrior. (l. 26)		
6 Stop that bawling, okay? (l. 30)		

7 WRITING What should a real friend be like?

_____ / 20

Your partner school writes about teenage topics in their school magazine every month.
This month's topic is the perfect friend.
Write a structured text for the school magazine giving your opinion on the question above.
Write about 180 words.

Write about

- what you look for in a friend
- what you like doing with a friend in your free time
- how important spending time together is to you
- topics you like to discuss with a friend
- other things that are important to you
- things a good friend should never do

8 WRITING Lots of problems

_____ / 20

Last night some of your friends sent you e-mails in which they told you about their problems.

Choose one of them and answer it. Write an e-mail of about 180 words.
Give some advice to your friend. Start and finish your e-mail in a friendly way.

…
I've failed an important exam and I don't know how to tell my parents. …

…
I saw a friend stealing money and I don't know who to tell. …

…
I saw my girlfriend flirting with my best friend. …

…
I want to go on a trip with my best friend, but my boyfriend doesn't want me to. …

9 WRITING A film I've watched

_____ / 20

Imagine you want to tell your English friend about a film you have watched recently.
Write an e-mail of about 150–180 words in which you tell your friend about the film.

Write

- its title
- what kind of film it is
- about the setting
- about the main characters
- where you watched it and who with
- what you liked / didn't like about it (actors, plot, special effects, soundtrack, ending, …)
- about your favourite or least favourite scenes

Say whether you would recommend watching it. Give reasons.

10 MEDIATION What is this film about?

_____ / 15

A friend in England wants to watch a German film. He has heard about the film "Renn, wenn du kannst". Read about the film and explain in English what it is about.

Write
- about the main characters (8)
- about the plot (5)
- a general comment about the film / qualities that make the film special (2)

Renn, wenn du kannst

Der Student Ben (Robert Gwisdek) sitzt querschnittsgelähmt im Rollstuhl und ist auf Betreuung angewiesen. Er schikaniert seine Mutter und auch die ihm zugeteilten Zivildienstleistenden. Sein neuer Zivi Christian (Jacob Matschenz), ein lebenslustiger Medizinstudent, gibt ihm Kontra und lässt sich nicht von seinen Befehlen beeindrucken. Sie werden sogar Freunde.

Eines Tages begegnet ihnen die Musikstudentin Annika (Anna Brüggemann). Beide verlieben sich in sie. Annika ist hin- und hergerissen: Zunächst fühlt sie sich zu dem fröhlichen Christian hingezogen. Ben glaubt, keine Chance bei ihr zu haben. Er geht davon aus, als Körperbehinderter im Rollstuhl nicht attraktiv für sie zu sein. Doch dann kommt es anders. Er und Annika kommen sich näher. Zwischen ihnen entwickelt sich eine Beziehung, die sie an ihre emotionalen Grenzen stoßen lässt, aber auch den Impuls versetzt, über sich hinauszuwachsen.

In diesem Film über Freundschaft, Liebe und Sexualität vor dem sensiblen Thema der Körperbehinderung kommt Humor nicht zu kurz. Die Darsteller bringen mit ihren witzigen Dialogen Leichtigkeit und Komödiantisches in die schwierige Dreiecksbeziehung.

11 MEDIATION I've got mail

_____ / 10

Dein amerikanischer Brieffreund Eric hatte geplant, dich in den Sommerferien zu besuchen. Nun erhältst du eine E-Mail, in der er dir seine Situation schildert und erklärt, warum er nicht zu Besuch kommen kann.

Erkläre deinem Vater
- Erics Situation (2)
- wie Eric die Situation sieht (3)
- was Erics Eltern darüber denken (5)

To: justinL15@hotmail.com
Cc:
Subject: summer holidays

Hi …

I've got some really bad news. Guess, what happened to me. I'm grounded. Last week we got our school reports and I got an F in Math. Well, as you know, I've always had problems with Math, but I've worked really hard. I often did my homework with Alex who is our Math expert. No, I didn't copy from him, we did it together and he helped me. I also asked my Math teacher for help but he refused any support. He said I didn't pay attention in his lessons.

Anyway, the last two months everything went wrong and my parents don't believe me. They think I didn't work hard enough. They say I hung out with my friends too often and now they don't believe Alex and I met to work. They want me to repeat the year. But that isn't all. They also expect me to attend a Math course in summer and won't let me visit you in Germany. I've tried talking to them and said that I'll revise Math as soon as I'm back from Germany but they don't trust me. I'm really depressed and don't know what to do. If you have any ideas, please let me know.

Take care,
Eric

12 WORDS What a person can be or look like

a) *Find a word with the opposite meaning for the following adjectives.* ____/ 6

1 charming	
2 attractive	
3 fat	
4 hard-working	
5 mean	
6 curly (hair)	

b) *Find a word with the same meaning for the following adjectives.* ____/ 3

1 charming	
2 beautiful	
3 clever	

c) *Describe a person's appearance (face, hair, outfit) and character.* ____/ 10

It can be a friend, a classmate or someone from your family.
Use at least five of the adjectives from a) and b) and write at least five sentences.

13 WORDS Choose the right verb ____/ 4

Tick the right words to complete the sentences.

1 If you ________________ someone, you like him or her and want to go out with him or her.

a) ☐ meet b) ☐ fancy c) ☐ phone d) ☐ break up with

2 If I don't catch someone's telephone number, I ask him or her to ____________________ it.

a) ☐ repeat b) ☐ remember c) ☐ suggest d) ☐ mention

3 I missed the meeting because nobody had __________________ it to me.

a) ☐ explained b) ☐ mentioned c) ☐ supposed d) ☐ talked

4 I don't like going to parties because my boyfriend always ________________ with every girl there.

a) ☐ smiles b) ☐ kisses c) ☐ chats up d) ☐ flirts

14 WORDS Find the right words

a) *Find the right words.* ____/ 6

1 A person who writes articles to give his or her opinion about a new film or book: ______________

____

2 To hurt someone with your teeth: ______________

3 To tell someone that someone or something is good: ______________

4 Expecting a child: being ______________

5 Able to wait for a long time without becoming angry: ______________

6 Things such as sounds or lights in a film: ______________

b) *Explain the following words in English.* ____/ 8

1 environment: ______________

____

2 award: ______________

____

3 director of a film: ______________

____

4 review: ______________

____

c) *What verbs go with these nouns? Write down four verbs for each noun.* ____/ 8

exam: ______________

film: ______________

15 GRAMMAR Family photo

a) *In this photo you can see Mr Carter and his three children Sophie, Amanda and Leo.* ______/ 6

It's Wednesday evening.
Describe what everybody is doing.
Where are the children sitting?
Speculate where Mrs Carter is and what she is doing.
Write six sentences.

b) *Now look at the speech bubbles and write what the Carters usually do in the evening.* ______/ 6

Write six sentences.

Mr Carter:

Sophie:

c) *Now you: What do you and your family usually do in the evening?* ______/ 8

Write four sentences.

Übersicht der Aufgaben

Seite	Aufgabe	Kurzbeschreibung	Kompetenz	Punkte
25/26	1 **London's new bike hire scheme**	Informationen erfassen und *a)* Text 1: 8 Sätze in die richtige Reihenfolge bringen *b)* Text 2: Fragen kurz beantworten *c)* Text 3: Sätze vervollständigen	Hörverstehen I[1]	 8 6 8
27/28	2 **An audio guide**	Detailinformationen erfassen und *a)* eine Tabelle ausfüllen oder *b)* *Multiple-Choice*-Aufgaben lösen	Hörverstehen II[2]	 12 6
29	3 **It's hot today, isn't it?**	Einen Cartoon zum Thema *Klimawandel* mit Hilfe von Leitfragen beschreiben; über den eigenen Umgang mit der Umwelt sprechen	Monologisches Sprechen	20
29	4 **Holiday plans**	Mit Hilfe von Rollenkarten und Stichworten einen Dialog zum Thema *(umweltfreundliches) Reisen* führen	Dialogisches Sprechen	20
30–32	5 **Welcome to a year without garbage**	Detailinformationen erfassen und *a)* *Multiple-Choice*-Aufgaben lösen *oder* *b)* fehlende Informationen in eine Tabelle eintragen	Leseverstehen I[3]	 6 12
33–35	6 **Teenagers and technology**	Detailinformationen erfassen und *a)* Aussagen als *True/False/Not given* ankreuzen *oder* *b)* fehlende Informationen in eine Tabelle eintragen	Leseverstehen II	 10 14

[1] Die Hörtexte zu dieser Aufgabe wurden frei gesprochen anhand einer vorgegebenen Situation, d. h. ohne ausformulierte Textvorlage aufgenommen. Sie liegen deshalb nicht in schriftlicher Form vor.

[2] Das Transkript zum Hörtext zu dieser Aufgabe finden Sie als kostenloses Online-Angebot auf unserer Website **www.englishg.de** unter >Downloads<.

[3] Für die Bearbeitung dieser Aufgabe empfiehlt sich möglicherweise ein Wörterbuch.

Seite	Aufgabe	Kurzbeschreibung	Kompetenz	Punkte
36	7 **The importance of recycling**	Mit Hilfe einer Illustration zum Thema *Müllproduktion* über eigene Bemühungen, die CO_2-Bilanz zu verbessern, schreiben	Schreiben I[1]	20
36	8 **The Green Garbage Project**	Eine *written discussion* zum Thema *Müllvermeidung* schreiben	Schreiben II	20
37	9 **Stadtrad Hamburg**	Eine deutschsprachige Information über Leihfahrräder in Hamburg einem Austauschschüler auf Englisch erklären	Sprachmittlung I	16
38	10 **How to reduce your carbon footprint**	Eine englischsprachige Liste von Maßnahmen, die den CO_2-Ausstoß verringern, der Großmutter auf Deutsch erläutern	Sprachmittlung II	14
39	11 **Saving the planet**	Aus einer Auswahl jeweils das richtige Wort in Sätze einsetzen	Wortschatz I	10
40	12 **Appliances you use every day**	*a)* Wörter zu einer englischen Erklärung finden *b)* Einen Gegenstand aus dem alltäglichen Leben beschreiben	Wortschatz I	5 8
40	13 **In the past and now**	*a)* Verben im *simple past* oder *simple present* in einen Lückentext einsetzen *b)* Anhand von Stichworten Sätze über den Gebrauch alltäglicher Gegenstände früher und heute schreiben	Grammatik	13 8

[1] Dieses Bild in Farbe finden Sie als kostenloses Online-Angebot auf unserer Website **www.englishg.de** unter >Downloads<.

1 LISTENING London's new bike hire scheme 5, 6, 7

a) Text 1 5

Read the sentences below. Then listen to the text and put them in the correct order. ____/ 8

☐ **A** The bike is quite heavy so he can't cycle fast.

☐ **B** After choosing a bike he unlocks it.

☐ **C** He goes to the docking station and finds a lot of bikes there.

☐ **D** There is a docking station near his office where he can drop off his bike.

☐ **E** Then he checks if everything is working.

☐ **F** The reporter has arrived at Waterloo station by train from Woking.

☐ **G** London's mayor hopes that the new scheme will help to reduce air pollution in the city.

☐ **H** He wants to try out the new bike hire scheme to get to his office.

b) Text 2 6

Miguel and Maria are from Spain. They are on holiday in London and Randeep Rawat is asking them what they think about cycling in London.

Look at the questions. Then listen to the text and write down what they like or don't like. ____/ 6

1 What do they like about cycling in London? (Name **two** facts.)

____

____

2 What was not easy for them when they were cycling in London? (Name **four** facts.)

____

____

____

____

c) Text 3 7

Randeep Rawat talks about how the new London bike hire scheme works.

Read the task. Then listen to the text and finish the sentences.
You will hear the recording twice. ______/ 8

1 The bikes are easy to recognize because ______________________________

2 To hire a bike you can register ______________________________

3 Then you are given ______________________________

4 You can use that for ______________________________

5 If you are not a member, you can ______________________________

6 The bikes should be used for short journeys in the city so ______________________________

____

7 There is a team of mechanics to ______________________________

8 If the new bike scheme is successful, it will grow and will help to make London ______________________________

____

2 LISTENING An audio guide 8

a) *There are four generations of mobile phones. Read the task. Then listen to the text and complete the chart with the missing information.* ______ / 12

1 Cell technology: invented when?	______
2 First generation: when? 3 Used where?	______ ______
4 Second generation: when? 5 How heavy? 6 First SMS text message:	______ ______ *a)* Where? ______ *b)* When? ______
7 Third generation: when? 8 What can they do? (Name **two** facts.)	______ *a)* ______ *b)* ______
9 Fourth generation: what will they be able to do? (Name **two** facts.)	*a)* ______ *b)* ______

OR

b) *Read the task. Then listen to the text and tick the correct ending.* ______/ 6

1 The cell technology that was used in mobile phones	*a)* was developed in the last decade.	
	b) was successful in cars too.	
	c) was invented in the 1940s.	
	d) has been used for the past twenty years.	
2 In 1908 people started to do experiments with radio phones	*a)* in cars and on ships.	
	b) in planes.	
	c) on trains and buses.	
	d) on boats.	
3 The mobile phones used in the early 1980s	*a)* were installed on ships.	
	b) needed a lot of batteries.	
	c) were cheap.	
	d) were as big as a briefcase.	
4 The digital technology in the 1990s made mobile phones	*a)* cheaper and lighter.	
	b) lighter and bigger.	
	c) quicker and more reliable.	
	d) more fashionable and lighter.	
5 Since the mid 2000s mobile phones have not only been used for making phone calls but also	*a)* for sending text messages and playing games.	
	b) for checking e-mails and for instant messaging.	
	c) for checking e-mails and taking photos.	
	d) for playing games and taking photos.	
6 The fourth generation has only just come on the market. These mobile phones	*a)* will be even faster and better on the internet.	
	b) will send text messages much faster.	
	c) will be much more expensive.	
	d) will allow you to watch videos.	

3 SPEAKING It's hot today, isn't it?

_____/ 20

- *Describe the cartoon and say what you think its message is.*
- *Have you ever experienced extreme weather conditions? (What? / When? / Where?)*
- *Do you and your family talk about environmental problems?*
- *Do you try to live in an "environment-friendly" way? (Describe how.)*

Start talking when you are ready and talk for about five minutes.

4 SPEAKING Holiday plans

_____/ 20

Your family is making plans for next year's holidays. Your parents have asked you and your brother/sister to think about where you want to go, what you want to do there and how you want to get there.

Look at the role cards and talk to your brother/sister. Think of other reasons that can help your partner to agree with your ideas.
Prepare a dialogue of about five to seven minutes. You've got ten minutes to prepare it.

Partner A

Discuss where you want to go and what you want to do there.

You don't want to fly, but want to go by car or train or bike.

Say why you don't want to fly (too expensive / too much pollution, …).

Say that you can see interesting/funny/… things on your way.

Partner B

Discuss where you want to go and what you want to do there.

You want to fly.

Say why you want to fly (fast/far away/…).

Say why you don't want to go by car, train or bike (takes too long / can't go to all the interesting places; by bike – can't take many things with you …).

5 READING Welcome to a year without garbage

Green Garbage Project

Home

Welcome to the official website of the 2009–2010 Green Garbage Project. This site will chronicle a year in which a (fairly) typical American married couple endeavors to live for a year without throwing away … well, anything. Impossible, you say? We don't think so, but we aim to find out.

CHALLENGE DETAILS

WHAT is the Green Garbage Project?

The Green Garbage Project is pretty simple, really. It's a little like a science experiment, where we start out with a question: Is it possible to live for one year without producing trash that winds up in a landfill? With a few minor exceptions, we think this is possible, even living in the country that produces more trash each year than any other country in the world. So, we set out to answer the question by putting our own lifestyle to the test. For one year, we will produce as little trash as humanly possible – ultimately, we hope to produce one plastic grocery sack (or less) of garbage bound for the landfill.

I'm not going to pretend it's going to be easy, especially when it comes to our young nephews visiting us this summer, Christmas, eating out, grocery shopping, our trip to Ashland and Crater Lake, etc. In fact, this project will touch every part of our lives. It will mean planning ahead, researching recycling facilities and packaging products, and lots of extra time and effort, but we believe that, in the end, it will be worth it.

Why are we doing this?

The statistics speak for themselves – the average U.S. citizen produces 4.5 pounds of garbage a day, more than anywhere else in the world. 16,000 plastic bags are used each second in the United States. Americans recycle only about 32 % of our total waste. And the big one – 99 % of everything that we buy ends up trashed within six months. Does this make sense to anybody?

We believe that, somewhere, society took a wrong turn, environmentally-speaking. We use up our natural resources faster than the earth can replenish them, and we've become a throwaway society. This feels unnatural, wasteful and dirty.

We also believe that, intrinsically, the earth is worth saving – for future generations and for the sake of preserving the natural beauty of the outdoors, which we have all had occasion to marvel at before. So, we became members of what is now called the Green Movement. We became environmentally conscious, making an effort, at least, to buy local, organic, cruelty-free, and fair-trade products, to buy biodegradable cleaning products, to recycle, and to use green bags for carrying purchases whenever possible. But no matter what we did, it never felt like we were making an appreciable difference. The trash still piled up, landing in a dump somewhere to stagnate for years to come.

Finally, we decided that enough is enough. The Green Garbage Project is our way to make a difference. We also hope it can help us answer some of those nagging, trash-related environmental questions. Will it solve all the world's problems? No, of course not – but this way we can see a difference in our personal environmental impact. This is our own personal way to tread lightly. If each American produces 4.5 pounds of garbage a day, that's more than 1,600 pounds of garbage per person a year, and 3,200 pounds of garbage between us. If we can reduce that number to 800 pounds, 400 pounds, or hopefully even 4.5 pounds in a year's time, then we've made an appreciable difference – and maybe inspired other people to do the same.

Source: http://greengarbageproject.adammathiasdesign.com/

a) Read the text and tick the correct ending. ____/ 6

1 Living without producing trash for one year	a) is not possible because the country produces so much trash.	
	b) is possible although you have to make a few exceptions.	
	c) is possible but you have to answer a lot of questions before starting.	
2 It won't be easy for the American couple because they	a) have to visit their friends in the summer.	
	b) are staying at home this Christmas.	
	c) have their young nephews staying in the summer.	
3 Before starting the project the couple have to	a) find recycling activities.	
	b) plan a lot of things very carefully.	
	c) unpack the products they have bought at the grocery store.	
4 Statistics for the USA say that	a) 4.5 pounds of garbage is produced by most of the US citizens per day.	
	b) US citizens recycle all their plastic bags.	
	c) most of the things that are bought will be thrown away within a year.	
5 Members of the Green Movement try to	a) buy as many recycled products as they can.	
	b) buy products that are produced locally.	
	c) use green bags at least twice.	
6 The Green Garbage Project is a way to	a) answer some of the most important environmental questions.	
	b) reduce the amount of garbage produced every day to 1000 pounds.	
	c) change everybody's environmental impact.	

OR

b) *Find the missing information in the text and complete the table.*
Give short answers or write numbers.

_____ / 12

1 Name **five** reasons why it is difficult to take part in the Green Garbage Project	1 ______ 2 ______ 3 ______ 4 ______ 5 ______
2 Number of plastic bags used each second in the USA	
3 Percentage of waste that is recycled in the USA	
4 Name **four** things members of the Green Movement do for the environment	1 ______ ______ 2 ______ ______ 3 ______ ______ 4 ______ ______
5 Amount of garbage a person produces every year in the USA	

6 READING Teenagers and technology

The following texts are excerpts from an article in the British newspaper "The Guardian" about teenagers and the way they use their mobile phones and the internet.

by **Jon Henley**

First, 75% of all teenagers (and 58% of 12-year-olds) now have a mobile phone. Almost 90% of phone-owning teens send and receive texts, most of them daily. Half send 50 or more texts a day; one in three sends 100. In fact, in barely four years, texting has established itself as comfortably "the preferred channel of basic communication between teens and their friends".

But phones do more than simply text, of course. More than 80% of phone-owning teens also use them to take pictures (and 64% to share those pictures with others). 60% listen to music on them, 46% play games, 32% swap videos and 23% access social networking sites. The mobile phone, in short, is now "the favoured communication hub for the majority of teens".

As if texting, swapping, hanging out and generally spending their waking hours welded to their phones wasn't enough, 73% use social networking sites, mostly Facebook – 50% more than three years ago. Digital communication is not just prevalent in teenagers' lives. It IS teenagers' lives.

Philippa Grogan, aged 16, reckons she sends "probably about 30" text messages every day, and receives as many. "They're about meeting up – where are you, see you in 10, that kind of thing," she says. "An awful lot of flirting goes on, of course. Or it's, 'OMG, what's biology homework?'. And, 'I'm babysitting and I'm SOOOO bored.'" (Boredom appears to be the key factor in the initiation of many teen communications.)

Like most of her peers, Philippa wouldn't dream of using her phone to actually phone anyone, except perhaps her parents – to placate them if she's not where she should be, or ask them to come and pick her up if she is. Calls are expensive, and you can't make them in class (you shouldn't text in class either, but "lots of people do").

Philippa also has 639 Facebook friends, and claims to know "the vast majority" (though some, she admits, are "quite far down the food chain"). "I don't want to be big-headed or anything, but I am quite popular," she says. "Only because I don't have a social life outside my bedroom, though." When I call her, 129 of her friends are online.

Facebook rush-hour is straight after school, and around nine or 10 in the evening. "You can have about 10 chats open at a time, then it gets a bit slow and you have to start deleting people," Philippa says. The topics? "General banter, light-hearted abuse. Lots of talk about parties and about photos of parties." Cred-wise[1], it's important to have a good, active Facebook profile: lots of updates, lots of photos of you tagged. Sometimes, though, it ends in tears. Everyone has witnessed cyber-bullying, but the worst thing that happened to Philippa was when someone posted "a really dreadful picture of me, with an awful double chin", then refused to take it down. "She kept saying, 'No way, it's upped my profile views 400%,'" says Philippa. It's quite easy, she thinks, for people to feel "belittled, isolated" on Facebook.

Source: http://www.guardian.co.uk/lifeandstyle/2010/jul/16/teenagers-mobiles-facebook-social-networking

[1] "cred" is an abbreviation of the word "credibility". It is a term used by teenagers to indicate acceptability amongst fashionable young people. The suffix "-wise" is used in English to form adjectives and adverbs, for example security-wise, money-wise. It is a synonym for "concerning" or "from the point of view of".

a) *Read the text. Then decide if the statements are true, false or not given.*
Tick the correct box.

_____ / 10

	True	***False***	***Not given***
1 More than half of all 12-year-old children in Britain own a mobile phone.			
2 About a third of all British teenagers with mobiles send 100 text messages.			
3 Four years ago they sent only 50 messages per day.			
4 More teenagers listen to music on their mobile phones than take photos with them.			
5 More boys than girls use their mobile phones to play games.			
6 Half of all British teenagers use social networking sites.			
7 Philippa Grogan gets about 30 text messages a day.			
8 Most teenagers prefer phoning because texting is more expensive.			
9 Philippa thinks she is quite popular because she has a lot of Facebook friends.			
10 Philippa had a bad experience with Facebook.			

OR

b) *Read the text. Find the missing information. Write numbers or give short answers.* _____/ 14

Teenagers and technology	
1 Teenagers owning a mobile phone (in %)	
2 Name **six** things teenagers do with their mobile phones	1 ______ 2 ______ 3 ______ 4 ______ 5 ______ 6 ______
3 Number of text messages Philippa gets per day	
4 Name **three** reasons for texting mentioned in the text	1 ______ 2 ______ 3 ______
5 Busiest times for using Facebook	1 ______ 2 ______
6 Worst thing that happened to Philippa on Facebook	

7 WRITING The importance of recycling

____/ 20

Here you see a garbage carbon footprint. Could it be yours?

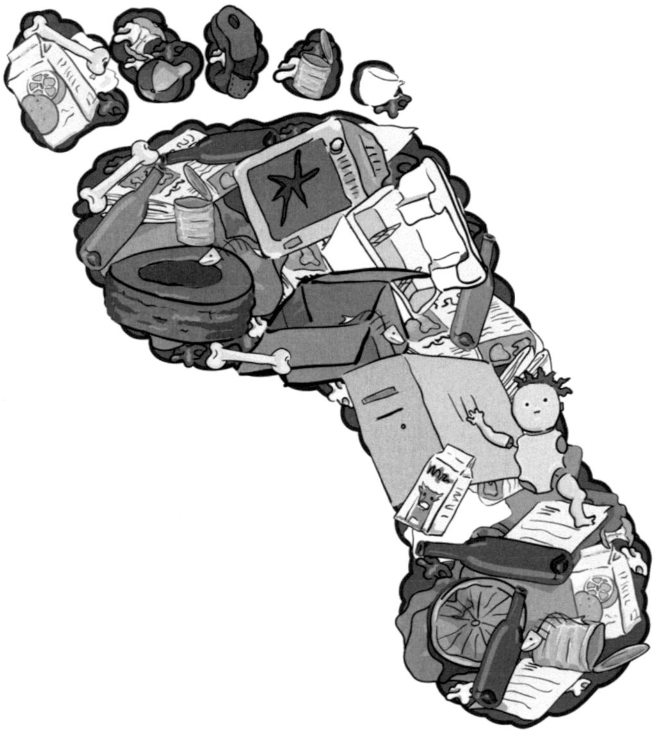

Write a text of about 160 words for your school magazine and say what you can do to reduce your garbage carbon footprint.

Think about

- home
- food
- school
- appliances
- transport

8 WRITING The Green Garbage Project

____/ 20

Your teacher has given you some statements and asked you to write a written discussion. This is your statement:

I am not going to take part in the Green Garbage Project because I don't think it will help us to save the planet.

Think about the outline of a written discussion and write a text of about 200 words.

9 MEDIATION Stadtrad Hamburg

_____ / 16

Ein amerikanischer Austauschschüler an deiner Schule möchte nach Hamburg fahren. Er hat gehört, dass man dort sehr leicht Fahrräder ausleihen kann. Du hast deine Tante, die in Hamburg lebt, gebeten, dir zu schreiben, wie das funktioniert. Ihre Antwort kam auf Deutsch.

Erkläre dem Austauschschüler auf Englisch:

- wie die Räder aussehen und wo man sie findet
- wie abgerechnet wird
- wie das Ausleihen und die Rückgabe funktionieren

To: Chrispinneberg15@hotmail.com
Cc:
Subject: Stadtrad Hamburg

Hallo Chris,

ich habe heute herausgefunden, wie das mit den Leihfahrrädern in Hamburg funktioniert:
Es gibt ca. 70 Leihstationen[1] über Hamburg verteilt. Eine ist direkt am Hauptbahnhof.
Die Fahrräder sind gut zu erkennen, weil sie alle rot lackiert sind.
Die ersten 30 Minuten sind kostenlos, dann wird im Minutentakt abgerechnet. Die Minute kostet zwischen 4 und 8 Cent.

Zum Ausleihen muss man durch Berühren den Touchscreen an der Station aktivieren und sich mit einer EC- oder Kreditkarte identifizieren.

Dann wählt man die Anzahl der Fahrräder, die man leihen möchte, indem man die angezeigten Fahrradnummern aktiviert. Anschließend erhält man einen Öffnungscode, den man ins Display des entsprechenden Fahrradschlosses eingibt[2]. Dann kann man losfahren.

Die Rückgabe ist genauso einfach. Man schließt das Fahrrad an einer Station an und drückt den Knopf am Fahrradschloss. Dann wird ein Quittungscode angezeigt, den man zusammen mit der Fahrradnummer eingeben muss. So erfährt man, wie viel man bezahlen muss.

Liebe Grüße!
Tante Petra

---

[1] Leihstation = *docking station*

[2] eingeben = *(to) key into / (to) type into*

10 MEDIATION How to reduce your carbon footprint

___ / 14

On the internet you have found ideas about how to reduce your carbon footprint.
You want to talk to your grandmother about these ideas but she does not understand English.
Look at the list and tell her in German what you want to do.

How to reduce your carbon footprint:

- buy recycled paper notebooks – it takes lots of water to make new paper
- turn off the water while you clean your teeth
- flush the toilet less often; don't use it as a bin
- reduce your shower time
- turn off the lights when you leave a room
- don't leave appliances on standby
- turn down the heating
- ask your parents to buy products in recyclable containers and to use newspaper to wrap presents
- climb stairs instead of using the lift – that keeps you fit

You Oma, guck mal hier sind Ideen, wie ich meine CO_2-Bilanz verringern kann. Ich lese dir mal die erste vor.

___

___

Oma Gibt es noch mehr Ideen zum Wassersparen?

You Ja, ___

___

___

Oma Das hört sich gut an. Wie kann man Energie sparen?

You ___

___

___

Oma Können Mama und Papa dir auch helfen?

You Ja, ___

___

Oma Das hört sich alles sehr sinnvoll an. Ist das alles?

You Nein, die beste Idee steht am Ende: ___

11 WORDS Saving the planet

_____ / 10

Read Laura Brown's diary and tick the correct word to complete the sentences.

Saturday, January 3rd

We sat down in the living room because Dad wanted to __________ us __________ the government online form to work out our family CO allowance.

1 a) ☐ take … through b) ☐ go … to c) ☐ bring … back

It's only two hours a day for electrical appliances. So we have to choose carefully – lights, toaster, __________ for some hot water for tea, and on and on …

2 a) ☐ hairdryer b) ☐ kettle c) ☐ fridge

Monday, January 5th

The carbon cards they sent us have got little blocks that go from green to red, and as you use your year's ration they disappear __________ till you are at the red one.

3 a) ☐ one and one b) ☐ one and two c) ☐ one by one

Thursday, January 8th

Mum and I went to the bus stop. When we walked past our car, she touched it with tears in her eyes. I __________ not to see.

4 a) ☐ pretended b) ☐ prepared c) ☐ presented

Then she couldn't find her carbon card and the people at the bus stop got quite angry. She said she felt __________ for her generation because they had messed things up for us.

5 a) ☐ ridiculous b) ☐ responsible c) ☐ represented

I was late for school because I had to swipe my CO card at the gate but the machine kept __________.

6 a) ☐ breaking down b) ☐ beating up c) ☐ breaking up

Tuesday, January 13th

Dad spends all night on his laptop, Mum is lost on a bus somewhere and Kim just stays in her room – an __________ ball of silence.

7 a) ☐ bad b) ☐ ugly c) ☐ evil

Wednesday, January 14th

When I woke up this morning, it was __________. I am only allowed to heat my room between 7 and 8.

8 a) ☐ hot b) ☐ rainy c) ☐ freezing

Dad keeps the bedroom temperature at 15 °C – that's not even enough to __________ the ice on the windows.

9 a) ☐ melt b) ☐ meet c) ☐ break

Tuesday, January 20th

It is still cold. The house feels even colder this morning because we had a __________ last night.

10 a) ☐ energy problem b) ☐ cold problem c) ☐ power cut

12 WORDS Appliances you use every day

a) *Find the correct words.* ____/ 5

1 You use it to operate a television or stereo from a distance. ____________________

2 You put this into an electric lamp or appliance to give light. ____________________

3 You use it to warm or cook food quickly. ____________________

4 You turn it on when it is cold in the house. ____________________

5 You use it when the battery of your mobile is weak. ____________________

b) *Are there **other** appliances you use every day?* ____/ 8

*Choose **one** and write a short text about it.*

Say
- what it is
- what you use it for
- why you use it every day
- if you could or couldn't live without it

13 GRAMMAR In the past and now

a) *Fill in the correct form of the verbs. Use the simple present or the simple past.* ____/ 13

In the past people ____________________ (write) letters to communicate with others. Today they ____________________ (send) e-mails.

Today people ____________________ (produce) environment-friendly cars. In the past they ____________________ (not care) about the CO_2 emission of cars.

When the walkman was invented, people ____________________ (listen) to music on the way to work or while they were running in the park. Today they ____________________ (use) an MP3 player to do this.

Now children ____________________ (play) games on games consoles. In the past they ____________________ (go) outside and ____________________ (play) in the park.

When people ____________________ (not find) their way in a foreign city, they ____________________ (use) maps or ____________________ (ask) people for directions. Today they ____________________ (switch on) their GPS.

b) *Look at the words below and write four sentences about what people did in the past and what they do now.* ____/ 8

telephone – phone people	→ send text messages	holidays – car or train	→ go by plane
news – listen to radio	→ watch on TV	books – read	→ listen to audiobooks

Have your say!

Unit 3

Übersicht der Aufgaben

Seite	Aufgabe	Kurzbeschreibung	Kompetenz	Punkte
43	1 **Webcast: Stanley Park School**	Informationen erfassen und sechs Fragen kurz beantworten	Hörverstehen I[1]	10
44	2 **The National Youth Rights Association**	Detailinformationen erfassen und in Stichworten in eine Tabelle eintragen	Hörverstehen II	12
45	3 **Young people and politics**	Mit Hilfe einer Grafik über Jugendliche und ihr Interesse an Politik sprechen	Monologisches Sprechen	20
46	4 **A discussion with your host family**	Mit Hilfe von Rollenkarten und einer Werbeanzeige eine Diskussion über die Überwachung mit Hilfe des Handys führen	Dialogisches Sprechen	20
47/48	5 **Award for teenager who nursed her dying friend**	Einen Zeitungsartikel lesen und *a)* Kurzantworten auf Fragen geben *b)* eine E-Mail an einen Freund schreiben	Leseverstehen I Schreiben	 11 20
49/50	6 **The UK Youth Parliament**	Detailinformationen erfassen und in Stichworten in eine Tabelle eintragen	Leseverstehen II[2]	11
51/52	7 **Jane Goodall's Roots & Shoots**	Einen Text einer Website lesen und *Multiple-Choice*-Aufgaben lösen	Leseverstehen III[2]	8
53	8 **Young and old drivers**	Mit Hilfe einer Statistik zu Unfällen von Fahrern unterschiedlichen Alters einen Artikel für die Schülerzeitung schreiben	Schreiben I	20
54	9 **Teenage drinking**	Einen Leserbrief zum Thema *Alkohol* schreiben	Schreiben II	20
54	10 **Travelling alone**	Eine englischsprachige Reiseinformation den Eltern auf Deutsch erläutern	Sprachmittlung I[2]	12

[1] Die Transkripte der Hörtexte zu dieser Unit finden Sie als kostenloses Online-Angebot auf unserer Website **www.englishg.de** unter >Downloads<.
[2] Für die Bearbeitung dieser Aufgabe empfiehlt sich möglicherweise ein Wörterbuch.

Seite	Aufgabe	Kurzbeschreibung	Kompetenz	Punkte
55	11 **Wahlen zum Jugendparlament**	Einem amerikanischen Austauschschüler die Wahlen zum Jugendparlament auf Englisch erklären	Sprachmittlung II	8
56	12 **Speak out!**	Aus einer Liste die richtigen Wörter in Sätze einordnen	Wortschatz I	6
56	13 **Explaining words**	*a)* Umschriebene Wörter finden und aufschreiben *b)* Vorgegebene Wörter umschreiben	Wortschatz II	5 10
57	14 **A school project**	In einem Text die jeweils richtige Präposition unterstreichen	Grammatik I	14
58	15 **Youth Conference**	In einen Text die jeweils richtige Formulierung aus einer Auswahl einsetzen	Grammatik II	8

1 LISTENING Webcast: Stanley Park School 🎧 9

Read the questions below. Then listen to the Stanley Park School webcast and answer the questions. You will hear the recording twice. ____ / 10

1 What does the school want to buy with the money they get for selling the school field?

____

2 What is the place used for at the moment? ______________________________

3 What will the problem be for the hockey team if the field is sold? ______________________________

____

4 What could the new IT block be used for? (Name **two** things.) ______________________________

____

____

5 Why can't George work on the computer at home? (Give **two** reasons.) ______________________________

____

____

6 What has Paul Austin already done or what is he planning to do to make sure the field is not sold? (Name **three** things.) ______________________________

____

____

2 LISTENING The National Youth Rights Association 10

Matt and Sarah are volunteers at the National Youth Rights Association. They travel around schools.

Listen to them and fill in the missing information in the grid below in no more than five words. You will hear the recording twice.

_____ / 12

0 Name of organization (example)	National Youth Rights Association
1 Reason for travelling around schools	
2 The NYRA's aim	
3 Number of NYRA members	
4 Name **two** things the NYRA is focusing on at the moment	1 ______ 2 ______
5 Name **two** situations where young people are treated like adults	1 ______ 2 ______
6 Name **one** situation where young people are not treated like adults	
7 Name **two** things NYRA volunteers do	1 ______ 2 ______
8 Name **two** things people who are interested in the NYRA can do	1 ______ 2 ______

3 SPEAKING Young people and politics

_____/ 20

Look at the charts about teenagers and their attitude towards politics. Prepare a talk about this topic. In this talk answer the questions below. You have got five minutes to prepare it. You may make notes.

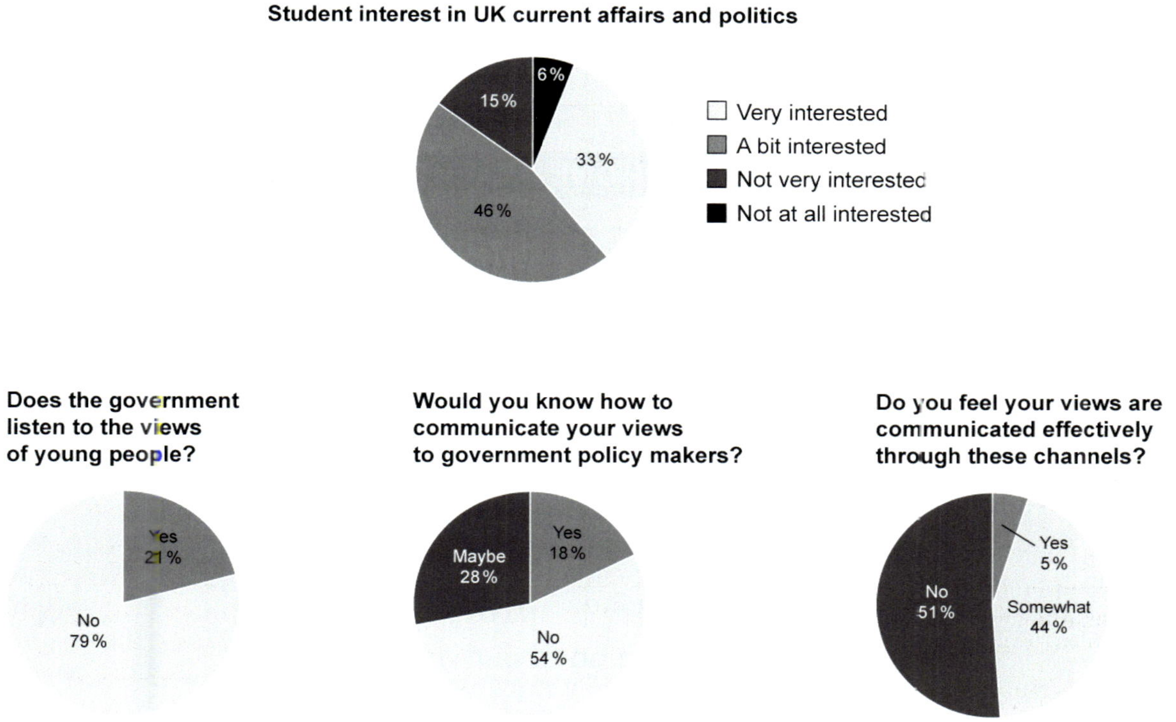

Source: http://insight.thestudentroom.co.uk/126/where-are-all-the-young-people-in-politics/ (March 2010)

- How interested are young people in politics and how involved do they feel in decisions made by the government? Use the information from the charts.
- What do you and your friends think about politics? Is it similar to the majority of the young people asked in the survey?
- How do things have to be changed to make it easier for young people to get involved? What benefits or dangers would there be if young people had more rights in politics?
- Would you personally like to get (more) involved? Why or why not?

4 SPEAKING A discussion with your host family

____/ 20

The following advert is from an English magazine for parents. Of course, teenagers and parents have different opinions about it.

Act out the role play below together with your partner. Read the article and your role card. Start talking when you're ready and keep the conversation going for about five minutes.

MOBILE PHONE TRACKING

Worried about your child's or teenager's safety?

We've got the solution to your problem.

Our new tracking device makes it possible for parents to find out where their child is at any time.

It is so easy. You simply install our software on your computer and on your child's mobile phone.

Whenever you log on to our website, you'll be able to see where your child is.

Partner A

You are sixteen years old. You are taking part in an exchange programme in England for a month. Your host family, the Browns, are worried about you. That's why they suggest using mobile phone tracking.

You do not like the idea. Discuss with Mr/Mrs Brown.

You start the conversation. Remember to be polite.

Partner B

You are Mr/Mrs Brown. An exchange student from Germany is spending one month with you and your family. He/She is sixteen years old. You are really worried about him/her. That's why you want to use mobile phone tracking.

Your exchange student does not like this idea and wants to discuss it with you.

5 READING Award for teenager who nursed her dying friend

Read the newspaper article. Then answer the questions below.

by **Genevieve Roberts**

AN A-LEVEL student turned her bedroom into a "hospital" to care for her best friend as he was dying from cancer.

Sophie Hartwell, 18, nursed Chris Day, 17, during his last month of life. She stayed up all night, talking to him and playing games to distract him when he was too scared to sleep.

She said: "We were best friends and spent every day together. When Chris was diagnosed with cancer last August, the first person he told was me. Even when he was so ill, he kept smiling."

Chris had a kidney removed and underwent chemotherapy. Having been in care from the age of 10, Chris, who like Sophie was studying A-level psychology, sociology and law, had no links with his birth parents and spent Christmas with the Hartwell family in Mitcham. Sophie, who attends John Ruskin College in Croydon, said: "He was really poorly, but he still enjoyed Christmas. My mum got him a stocking, just like me and my sisters, and he was made feel part of the family."

Sophie, who met Chris when they started sixth form together, is among 70 inspirational young people from England and Wales who were each receiving a Diana Award – named after Diana, Princess of Wales – from Schools Minister Nick Gibb today.

By Boxing Day, Chris' condition deteriorated and Sophie's mother Michelle, 44, took him to the Royal Marsden. "He was there over New Year," said Sophie. "The cancer had spread. Chris had a meeting with the hospital consultants in January and they told him he may not make it to the weekend. He didn't want to die in hospital, so he came to my house. And he stayed for a month, dying on February 27."

Sophie said she could not have looked after her friend so well without the support of her mother, and two sisters, Amy, 16, and Maisie, 13. "I shared my bedroom with Chris," she said. "We had five oxygen tanks, to help him breathe, and I knew his medication off by heart because I was responsible for making sure he took it.

"I helped him to organize a big party at Croydon aerodrome before he died, calling all his friends and arranging a minibus and cake. And I helped to organize his funeral. He was one of the nicest people you could ever meet, so loud, intelligent and funny."

Source: Evening Standard 28 June 2010

a) *Answer the questions in 1–5 words or numbers.* ____/ 11

Award for teenager who nursed her dying friend	
1 What did Sophie do for Chris during the last weeks of his life? Name **three** things.	1 ________ 2 ________ 3 ________
2 When was Chris diagnosed?	
3 What was the diagnosis?	
4 What did Sophie's mum do to make Chris feel part of the family? Name **two** things.	1 ________ 2 ________
5 Where did Sophie get to know Chris?	
6 Who gave the Diana Award to Sophie?	
7 What is the name of the hospital Chris got treated in?	
8 Where did Chris die?	

b) *After you have read the article above, you feel an award for young people who help others is a very good idea. You would like to start a campaign like this in Germany. You decide to write an e-mail to a friend to ask him/her for help.* ____/ 20

Write about 150 words.

- Include general information about the article.
- Say what you think the advantages of an award like the 'Diana Award' are.
- Suggest other things young people could do to receive an award like this.
- Ask your friend for his or her opinion and ideas for your campaign.

6 READING About the UK Youth Parliament

____/ 11

UK Youth Parliament (UKYP)

Home

- Home
- Contact us
- About us

The UK Youth Parliament (UKYP) enables young people to use their energy and passion to change the world for the better. Run by young people for young people, UKYP provides opportunities for 11–18-year-olds to use their voice in creative ways to bring about social change.

The UK Youth Parliament has 600 elected Members of Youth Parliament (MYPs) aged 11–18. MYPs are elected in annual[1] youth elections throughout the UK. Any young person aged 11–18 can stand or vote. [...]

Once elected MYPs organize events and projects, run campaigns and influence decision-makers on the issues which matter most to young people. There are lots of ways for young people everywhere to get involved with the UK Youth Parliament, from supporting our campaigns to debating in our online forums. Maybe you even want to become an MYP yourself! For more information, go to www.ukyouthparliament.org.uk

Here's is an <u>overview</u> of some of the things we campaign for:

<u>Media Portrayal</u>
The negative stereotyping of young people in the media is unreasonable. To change this, UKYP want to encourage opportunities for positive press, on both a local and national scale. We believe young people should take a more active role in the media. We therefore encourage young people and media organizations to build a positive relationship, where the younger generation have a right of reply and can express themselves. [...]

<u>Jobs for young people</u>
UKYP believe that all young people (aged between 13 and 18) should have the opportunity to participate in work experience for a minimum of one week in a field of their choice. Each school should have a professionally trained and qualified careers adviser. [...]

Any advice given must be impartial and personalized. UKYP believes that jobs and volunteering opportunities for young people need to be more widely advertised in accessible places for young people.

<u>Bullying</u>
School anti-bullying policies should be written by students in consultation with teachers and relevant professionals. We believe that the policy should include:
- The necessity of having professional advice and support for both the victim and the bully.
- Schools should have better training for staff and advice for students.
- Action should be taken according to individual needs.

<u>Public Transport</u>
UKYP believe that young people should pay no more than ½ adult fare on public buses. [...]

More needs to be done to improve disabled access[2] and facilities on public transport.

<u>Child poverty</u>
[...] UKYP believes that no child should be in poverty. Every child matters and deserves a good quality of life. The Government have already set targets[3] to reduce child poverty, however these changes are said to be complete by 2020! UKYP argues that these targets should be met earlier and dealt with as soon as possible.

The Government's achievements so far have reduced children in extreme poverty to 1.7 million and from 1998–2007 600,000 children have been lifted from the poverty line. However some children remain behind. We believe that we can contribute to the Government's plans by trying to campaign for the target to end child poverty to be brought forward. [...]

Source: http://www.ukyouthparliament.org.uk/downloads/UKYP_Manifesto.pdf

[1] annual *jährlich* [2] access *Zugang* [3] (to) set targets *Zielvereinbarungen treffen*

Answer the following questions in 1–5 words or numbers.

1 How often are MYPs elected?	
2 How old are MYPs?	
3 What can you do if you want to get involved in the UKYP but not become an MYP?	1 ____________ 2 ____________
4 What **two** ideas does UKYP have for helping young people to find a suitable job?	1 ____________ 2 ____________
5 What does the UKYP advise students to write to fight against bullying?	
6 What **two** things does the UKYP want to be improved in public transport?	1 ____________ 2 ____________
7 When does the UKYP want the Government's targets on child poverty to be completed?	
8 How many children lived in extreme poverty in 2007?	

7 READING Jane Goodall's Roots & Shoots

_____ / 8

Read the text about the organization Roots & Shoots.

Roots and Shoots

Home

about us | news/events | campaigns | find a group | contact us | donate | store | search

What is *Roots & Shoots*?

Roots & Shoots is the Jane Goodall Institute's global environmental and humanitarian program for youth of all ages. It is a fun and exciting way for young people to identify problems and issues in their local communities and then discover ways to make the world a better place. All projects are focused on improving the lives of people, animals and the environment. Kids who belong to *Roots & Shoots* groups have the opportunity to network with *R&S* members from around the world to learn about other cultures and gain a deeper understanding of the global impact of their actions.

What makes *Roots & Shoots* different from other service organizations?

- History: Our roots are unique and special. We were founded by 12 Tanzanian students and Dr. Jane Goodall in 1991. We continue to be inspired by the leadership and legacy of Dr. Jane. Her pioneering idea that each individual can make a difference is the foundation of *Roots & Shoots*.
- Flexibility: Our learning model of knowledge, compassion and action provides a flexible structure for group activities, with room for seemingly endless creativity in application. Our members have formed *Roots & Shoots* groups in almost any context: classrooms, home school groups, families, neighbourhoods, community centers, zoos and nature centers, museums, 4-H clubs, scout troops, even prisons.
- International network: Hundreds of thousands of *Roots & Shoots* members in over 100 countries, make connections far beyond their home communities, fostering a better understanding of cultures and ecosystems.
- Youth-driven projects: We believe young people have the power to make a difference, and we offer our groups the tools and inspiration they need to plan and implement projects that are truly youth-led. We incorporate our young members' perspective into our regional and national strategic planning and foster leadership skills through opportunities such as the *Roots & Shoots* Youth Leadership Councils.

What are examples of typical projects?

Projects can be simple, individual efforts such as recycling your family's trash, or larger group efforts requiring a lot of people-power, like organizing to clean up a major urban park. How about holding a food or clothing drive or helping at an animal shelter? Many *Roots & Shoots* groups help out at local senior centers, plant butterfly gardens, build bird houses, educate others about endangered species or promote practices to reduce household energy use. Any project that helps the human community, preserves the lives of animals or improves the environment, fits within the *Roots & Shoots* goals. Our website includes project ideas and resources to help jump-start your ideas.

Get involved

Here are just two ideas of the type of projects you can organize. For more ideas visit the project database.

Host a Community Clean Up Day

All over the place, when we're walking to work, driving on the highway, it's pretty possible that you'll come across some litter. Whether it's cigarette butts, empty soda cans or plastic bags, it seems they're everywhere.

A community clean-up is a great way to get rid of these things, beautify the environment, increase civic pride and help animals.

Host a Movie Night

Invite your entire family over for a movie night with movies like *Food, Inc.*, or gather everyone up and go to a *Disneynature* movie. Find a place after the movie where you can discuss what you thought, and what actions you can take to help.

For more information, please visit www.rootsandshoots.org.

Source: http://www.rootsandshoots.org

Read the text and tick the correct statement.

1 Most projects are set	a) in Tanzania.	
	b) in the local communities of young people.	
	c) in classrooms.	
2 *R&S* have	a) a platform where young people get ideas for a new project.	
	b) large groups of people who come to local communities to support smaller groups.	
	c) an office which you can contact for project ideas.	
3 *R&S* were first started by	a) Dr. Jane.	
	b) 13 people.	
	c) the *R&S* Youth Leadership Council.	
4 *R&S* groups can be founded	a) by big groups of at least five people.	
	b) not only by young people but by adults too.	
	c) by different types of groups.	
5 People from	a) thousands of countries are registered at *R&S*.	
	b) more than one hundred countries are members of *R&S*.	
	c) almost all continents take part in *R&S* groups.	
6 *R&S* regularly	a) give an award to special projects.	
	b) ask their members to meet Dr. Jane.	
	c) listen to what young people think and give them the chance to speak out.	
7 Projects	a) can be anything that helps people, animals or the environment.	
	b) should involve more than just recycling your family's trash.	
	c) cannot take place at animal shelters.	
8 Movie nights	a) are a good way to get to know people.	
	b) can be an inspiration for project ideas.	
	c) should be for young people only.	

8 WRITING Young and old drivers

____ / 20

In the next issues of your school magazine you want to write about the topic of young drivers in Germany. You have found the chart below on a website. It shows the link between drivers' ages and the number of accidents in the USA. You would like to include the chart in your article.

Write the article of about 150 words for your school magazine. In your text:

- Write an introduction: Say something about when people are allowed to drive in Germany and in the USA.
- Give some information on age groups and the number of accidents they are involved in (use the information from the chart).
- Say what you think the consequences should be for drivers of certain age groups.

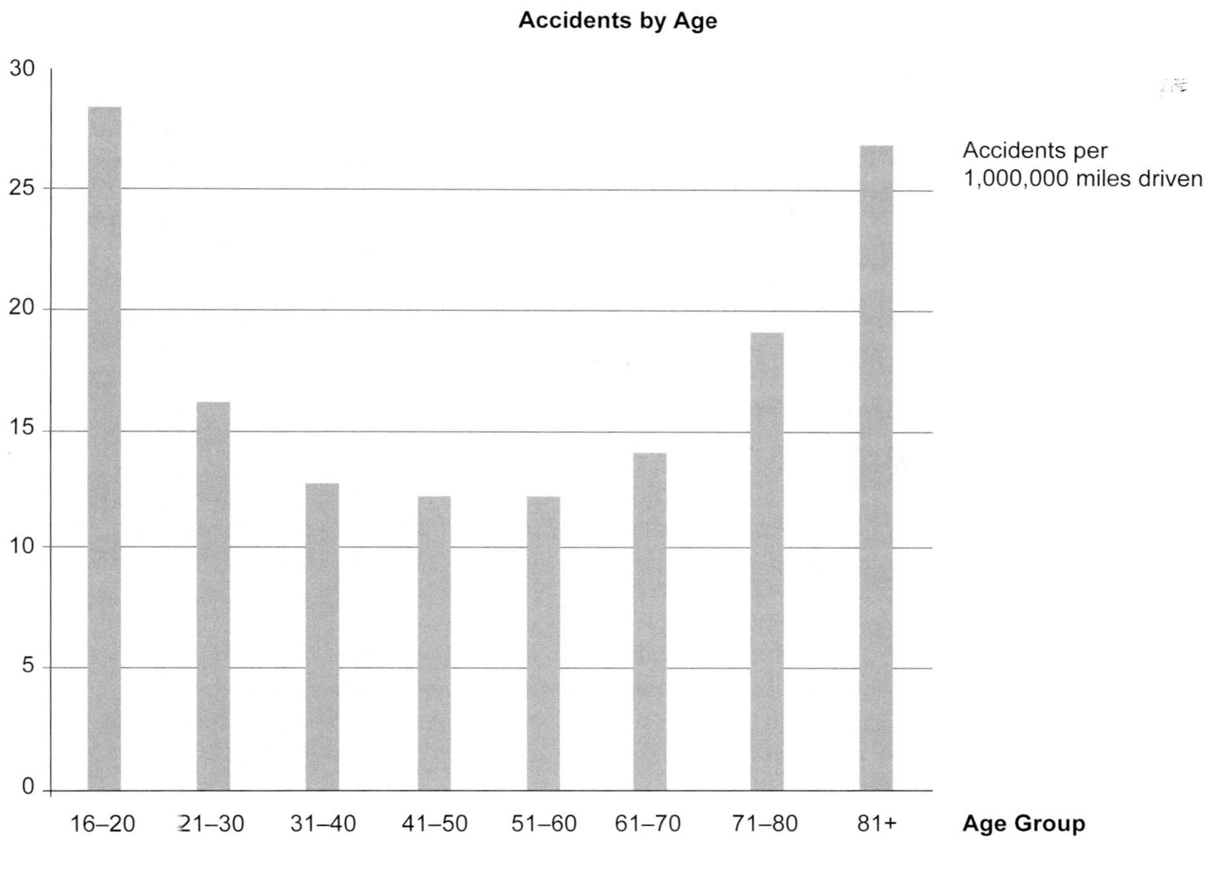

Source: http://www.qualityplanning.com/qpc_resources_public/news/030929-Older%20drivers_files/image003.gif

9 WRITING Teenage drinking

____/ 20

In an online magazine you read an article about young people and drinking. Authorities are now planning to make alcoholic drinks more expensive and non-alcoholic drinks cheaper to encourage young people to buy non-alcoholic drinks.

You are very interested in this topic and write a comment to the newspaper about it.
In your letter of about 150 words include:

- The reason for your letter.
- Your opinion about regulating the consumption of alcoholic drinks by making drinks cheaper/ more expensive. Give reasons for your opinion and/or say something about alternatives.
- Your experience with young people and drinking.

10 MEDIATION Travelling alone

____/ 12

Du planst mit deinem Freund Oliver aus England zusammen in den Urlaub zu fahren.
Ihr seid beide unter 18 und der englische Reiseveranstalter hat euch eine Broschüre geschickt, in der steht, was ihr und eure Eltern unbedingt beachten solltet. Deine Eltern bitten dich, ihnen auf Deutsch zu sagen, was in der Broschüre steht.

Teenage Travel Worldwide

Information for parents of teenage travellers without parents

Thousands of teenagers go on holiday without their parents every year and they have a great time.
As a tour operator, we have specialized in teenagers who travel without their parents.
Safety is taken very seriously by us. Below you find a list of things you and/or your child should consider before leaving:

- make sure your child knows the address of the nearest Embassy or Consulate in case of emergency
- get travel insurance and check that the cover is appropriate
- get a good guidebook to ensure they get to know their destination and find out about local laws and customs
- ensure they have a valid passport and make copies of it
- give them enough money for the trip and some back-up funds
- make sure they know how to contact you and you know how to contact them

11 MEDIATION Wahlen zum Jugendparlament

_____ / 8

An American exchange student is staying with you and your family. In your home town elections for the youth parliament are going to take place soon. Answer your friend's questions about them.

- What issues are discussed there? (2)
- Do you have to be in a political party in order to be elected? What else is important to become an active member? (2)
- Who can vote? (1)
- Where and when do the elections take place? (2)
- How often is a new parliament elected? (1)

Jugendparlament – Neuwahlen im Mai

Du möchtest deine Stadt kinder- und jugendfreundlicher machen?
Du willst dich in Politik einbringen und deine Meinung vertreten?

Dann nimm teil an der Wahl zum Jugendparlament!

Das Jugendparlament ist eine Gruppe Jugendlicher, die ihre Altersgruppe vertritt.
Wir sind ein Parlament. Allerdings spielen Parteien bei uns keine Rolle. Das Jugendparlament setzt sich besonders für die Interessen Jugendlicher ein, aber auch Themen, die alle Menschen etwas angehen, wie z. B. die Umwelt, liegen uns am Herzen.

Zur Wahl:

- Wählen können alle Kinder und Jugendlichen im Alter von 12–18 Jahren.
- Gewählt werden können alle Kinder und Jugendlichen zwischen 13 und 18 Jahren.
- Jeder Wahlberechtigte kann bis zu drei Stimmen abgeben. Dabei darf nur jeweils eine Stimme für eine Kandidatin oder einen Kandidaten abgegeben werden.
- Gewählt wird in den Schulen während der Schulpausen, in Freistunden oder nach Beendigung des Schulunterrichts.
- Das Parlament wird für 24 Monate gewählt und besteht aus 17 Mitgliedern.

12 WORDS Speak out!

_____/ 6

Put the words from the box into the correct gaps in the text. You might have to put them into the correct form. There are three more words than you need.

(to) care about • conflict • (to) criticize • (to) deserve • (to) improve • (to) make sense • sensible • (to) take action • vote

1 A lot of young people ______________________ the environment and try to save water and electricity.

2 Young people who ______________________ are not always easy to find because they often feel afraid of how adults will react.

3 Many young people ______________________ the government for strict rules about drinking or driving.

4 Young people often don't feel represented in Parliament. To ______________________ this situation they want the voting age to be lowered.

5 Many projects show that it ______________________ to listen to young people. They often have very good ideas.

6 They really ______________________ to have the same right to speak out as adults.

13 WORDS Explaining words

a) *Find out which words are described here and write them down.* _____/ 5

1 The place where town councillors work: ______________________

2 Another word for 'the same' (e.g. the same rights): ______________________

3 Someone who works in politics: ______________________

4 A person who helps when there is a conflict: ______________________

5 The UK head of government: ______________________

b) *Now explain these words.* _____/ 10

1 corridor: ______________________

2 tax: ______________________

3 political party: ______________________

4 (to) sign: ______________________

5 petition: ______________________

14 GRAMMAR A school project

_____/ 14

Underline the correct preposition.

Our environmental group YPSTE (Young People Save the Environment) is always looking **at** / **for** new members. That's why we are here. Maybe some of you would like to take part.

Our group was founded **in** / **on** 1986. Some teenagers started the idea **from** / **in** a school project. It all began with their teacher organizing a clean-up of the area **after** / **around** the school. Rose Pink and Trevor Bush were very enthusiastic right **for** / **from** the start. They gave interviews to the local press and even asked other people to get together in small groups in order to do clean-ups in a park or a forest.

Today YPSTE have about 100 members all **across** / **during** the city. We do not only do clean-ups these days. YPSTE members meet regularly to discuss local environmental issues. Very often we take part **at** / **in** demonstrations. Last month, when the expansion of the airport was being discussed, we organized a petition and met up **by** / **with** politicians who have a similar view **on** / **over** the expansion. The supporters of the expansion criticize us **about** / **for** our actions. But we believe that this is the only way to prevent the destruction of the forest **near** / **on** the airport where so many unique animals live.

So, if you are interested **for** / **in** joining us, please take a brochure and just come **by** / **to** our next meeting on Saturday. We are looking forward **over** / **to** seeing you there.

15 GRAMMAR Youth Conference

___/ 8

Choose the right expression for the numbered gaps and tick the answer in the table below.

At this month's Youth Conference, teenagers from all over the world are discussing issues like health, poverty, discrimination and environmental problems from their point of view. They are also looking **(1)** ___ the progress that has been achieved in the years **(2)** ___ their last Youth Conference in 2010. Young people know that since 2010 millions of young lives **(3)** ___: the number of child deaths has fallen rapidly within the past 10 years. More young people than ever are **(4)** ___ schools these days. However, too many children still die because medical care is not available to them. And too many of them **(5)** ___ a peaceful childhood.

The conference members do not think that enough has been done yet, but they have not lost hope. They **(6)** ___ that the goals of their conference held in 2010 are still possible. They point out that the world **(7)** ___ truly fit for children if action is taken by governments and also individuals, **(8)** ___ young people themselves.

1 a) ☐ to	b) ☐ for	c) ☐ at	d) ☐ after
2 a) ☐ around	b) ☐ for	c) ☐ from	d) ☐ since
3 a) ☐ are saved	b) ☐ have saved	c) ☐ have been saved	d) ☐ were saved
4 a) ☐ in	b) ☐ to	c) ☐ on	d) ☐ with
5 a) ☐ are experiencing	b) ☐ experience	c) ☐ hasn't got	d) ☐ will never experience
6 a) ☐ believe	b) ☐ lost	c) ☐ saw	d) ☐ were thinking
7 a) ☐ will only be	b) ☐ only be	c) ☐ is only	d) ☐ was only
8 a) ☐ although	b) ☐ including	c) ☐ for	d) ☐ or

Übersicht der Aufgaben

Seite	Aufgabe	Kurzbeschreibung	Kompetenz	Punkte
61	1 **Messages**	Informationen aus vier kurzen Ansagen erfassen und in eine Tabelle einfügen	Hörverstehen I[1]	14
62	2 **A job interview**	Detailinformationen erfassen und in eine Tabelle eintragen	Hörverstehen II[2]	13
63	3 **Future life**	Zwei gegensätzliche Sets von Fotos beschreiben und darüber sprechen, wie man sich die eigene Zukunft vorstellt	Monologisches Sprechen[3]	20
64	4 **Solving problems abroad**	Mit Hilfe von Rollenkarten über eine defekte Dusche in einer Jugendherberge sprechen und nach Lösungen suchen	Dialogisches Sprechen	20
65/66	5 **Jamie's blog: On safari in Kenya**	Einen Web Blog lesen und *a)* Aussagen als *True/False/Not given* ankreuzen *b)* Fakten in eine Tabelle eintragen *c)* mit Hilfe des Textes schreiben, ob man in Kenia Urlaub machen würde	Leseverstehen I Schreiben	 8 9 5
67/68	6 **Chapter 31**	Ein Kapitel aus dem Buch *The Curious Incident of the Dog in the Night-Time* lesen und *a)* acht Aussagen zum Text in die richtige Reihenfolge bringen *b)* drei Beispiele aus dem Text für Christophers Behinderung anführen	Leseverstehen II Schreiben	 8 3
69	7 **The story behind the picture**	Ein Foto beschreiben und über die Gefühle und Lebenssituation der Frau darauf spekulieren	Schreiben I	20

[1] Die Transkripte der Hörtexte zu dieser Aufgabe finden Sie als kostenloses Online-Angebot auf unserer Website **www.englishg.de** unter >Downloads<.
[2] Der Hörtext zu dieser Aufgabe wurde frei gesprochen anhand einer vorgegebenen Situation, d. h. ohne ausformulierte Textvorlage, aufgenommen. Er liegt deshalb nicht in schriftlicher Form vor.
[3] Diese Fotos in Farbe finden Sie als kostenloses Online-Angebot auf unserer Website **www.englishg.de** unter >Downloads<.

Seite	Aufgabe	Kurzbeschreibung	Kompetenz	Punkte
69	8 **Selling something on the internet**	Mit Hilfe einer Zeichnung eine Erfindung im Internet bewerben	Schreiben II	20
69	9 **Job advert**	Eine englischsprachige Stellenanzeige den Eltern auf Deutsch wiedergeben	Sprachmittlung I	12
70	10 **Das filmende Klassenzimmer**	Den Stundenplan eines Klassenausflugs in die Bavaria Filmstudios einem amerikanischen Gastschüler auf Englisch erläutern	Sprachmittlung II	12
71	11 **My first job**	In einem Text über Bewerbungsstrategien das jeweils richtige Wort unterstreichen	Wortschatz	10
71	12 **What is it?**	*a)* Umschriebene Wörter finden und aufschreiben *b)* Vorgegebene Wörter umschreiben	Wortschatz I	5 10
72	13 **Say it in English**	Situationen aus dem Alltagsleben auf Englisch wiedergeben	Wortschatz III	18
73	14 **At lunch break**	Mit Hilfe eines Bildes die richtigen Zeitformen (*simple present* oder *present progressive*) in Sätze einsetzen	Grammatik	14
74	15 **Technology has changed our lives**	In einem Text die jeweils richtige Zeitform (*simple present* oder *simple past*) unterstreichen	Grammatik I	14
74	16 **Future plans**	In verschiedene Aussagen *will* oder *won't* einsetzen	Grammatik III	6

1 LISTENING Messages 11, 12, 13, 14

_____/ 14

Read the tasks. Then listen to the texts and complete the table in 1–5 words or numbers.

Text 1, Message 1			
1 What does Mr Winter want to arrange with Laura?			
2 What days does he suggest meeting Laura?			
3 What's Mr Winter's telephone number?			
Text 1, Message 2			
4 What does Laura's mum want to know from her?			
Text 2			
1 What's the news for the A32 North?			
2 What has happened on the M27?			
3 Why has the train to London been cancelled?			
Text 3			
1 How long is the flight to Istanbul?			
2 Did the flight leave Munich on time?			
3 What time will the plane arrive in Istanbul?			
4 What is the weather like in Istanbul?			
Text 4			
Showing times for …			
1 *The Social Network*			
2 *Wall Street – Money Never Sleeps*			
3 *Despicable Me*			

2 LISTENING A job interview 15

_____/ 13

You are sitting in on an interview for a job at the Bluebell Café in Bath. Janet, the manager of the café, is doing the interview and has asked you to complete this form for each candidate. Read the form, then listen to the text and fill in or tick the information you hear.

0 Candidate's name	Antonella	
1 School and year		
2 Is the candidate interested in	*a)* a Saturday job?	
	b) a holiday job?	
	c) a Saturday job and a holiday job?	
3 Where did the candidate find out about the job?		
4 Experience as a waitress?		
5 Experience with food preparation? Where?		
6 What other qualities or qualifications does the candidate have?	1 ____________ ____________ 2 ____________ ____________	
7 The candidate asks about:	1 ____________ 2 ____________ 3 ____________ 4 ____________	

3 SPEAKING Future life

_____ / 20

Situation 1

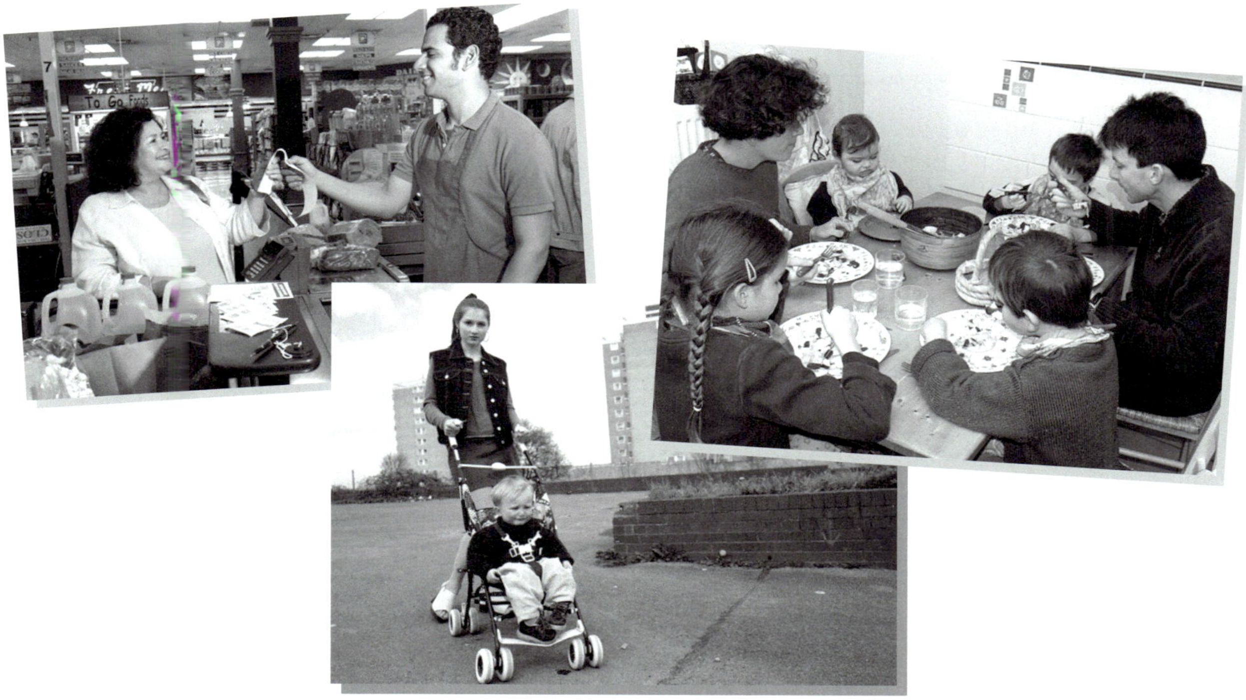

Situation 2

- *Look at your pictures. Describe the two different ways of life.*
- *Say what you like/don't like about them.*
- *Can you imagine your future life being like situation 1 or 2? Give reasons why or why not.*
- *What would you like your future life to be like?*

Speak for about five minutes.

4 SPEAKING Solving problems abroad

_____ / 20

Look at your role card and act out the conversation with your partner. Speak for about five minutes.

Partner A

You are staying in a youth hostel in London. It's the evening and you want to have a shower. You notice that there is a lot of water running from the showers into the hall. You go to the reception and tell the person there about the problem.

Find a way to solve the problem together.

- *Tell the receptionist about the problem with the water.*
- *Ask what you can do.*
- *React to the receptionist's ideas.*

Partner B

You are spending your summer holidays working as a receptionist in a youth hostel in London. A young person comes to the reception and tells you about a problem with the showers.

Find a way to solve the problem together.

- *Ask the guest where the water is and where it is coming from and say that you will send somebody to look at the problem.*
- *Point out alternatives (e. g. other showers in the hostel; showering the next morning).*
- *Be polite and apologize for the problem.*

5 READING Jamie's blog: On safari in Kenya

28 August: 21:38

Hi there everyone,

Got back from Kenya late yesterday evening – what a place! My two weeks there really were the holiday of a lifetime. I've posted some photos and videos for you to have a look at – check out the big cats! Dad had wanted to go to Africa for years and, as it was his 50th birthday this year, he decided we should go. Did you know that safari is the Swahili word for "journey"? Anyway, there were so many great things about the trip. Here are just some of the highlights:

Views of Mt Kilimanjaro

Our first stop after Nairobi was Amboseli, which is about four hours' drive from the capital. Amboseli is famous for its elephants and the views of Mount Kilimanjaro, Africa's highest mountain. Kilimanjaro is actually in Tanzania, but some of the best views are from Kenya. On our third day we got up really, really early to watch the sunrise over the mountain. I wasn't too happy when Mum woke me up and it was still dark, but the sunrise was magical – the colours were wonderful: purples and pinks.

The flamingos at Lake Nakuru

Lake Nakuru National Park is about 100 miles north of Nairobi. We spent an afternoon here looking at the flamingos. There are literally thousands of bright pink flamingos on the lake – so many that you can't see the lake itself. Absolutely awesome! The guide said that Lake Nakuru's flamingos are the most impressive bird spectacle on earth, and I can quite believe him.

Masai Mara National Reserve

The Masai Mara is where you go if you want to see the "Big 5", that is to say, the lion, the African elephant, the Cape Buffalo, the leopard and the rhinoceros. We stayed here for two days and did tours in the mornings, afternoons and at night. The night drive was so exciting! The driver told us lots of really interesting stories about the animals and the life of the Masai, the people who live in this region. He had a great sense of humour – Mum couldn't stop laughing! As you can see from the photos, we saw all of the "Big 5" on our trip – incredible! On the second evening we saw some Masai dancing and singing. You might have seen the Masai "jump dance" on television, but they have a lot more traditional dances than that. The most impressive thing about the music was that they don't use instruments – just their voices. My videos will give you an idea of what it was like, but they're nowhere near as good as the real thing.

I'd love to go back to Kenya. Several people told us how important tourism is for their country. After farming it is the second most important part of the Kenyan economy. We didn't have time, but a few people suggested we visit the beaches on the Indian Ocean too – they are supposed to be wonderful and I love the sea.

I hope you enjoy my photos – let me know what you think!
Jamie

a) *Are these sentences true, false or not in the text?* ____/ 8

	True	False	Not given
1 Jamie's dad only started thinking about going to Kenya last year.			
2 Safari means "journey" in Swahili.			
3 Thousands of tourists climb Kilimanjaro every year.			
4 The family didn't enjoy the safaris in the Masai Mara National Reserve.			
5 Jamie saw all of the "Big 5".			
6 They saw everything there is to see in Kenya.			
7 Holidays in Kenya are good value for money.			
8 Tourism is very important for Kenya.			

b) *Find the missing information in the text and complete the table.* ____/ 9

1 Reason for Jamie's visit to Kenya	
2 **Two** reasons why people visit Amboseli	1 ______ 2 ______
3 Reason for Jamie and his family getting up very early one morning	
4 Reason why the flamingos at Lake Nakuru are thought to be the most impressive bird spectacle on earth	
5 Reason why Jamie's mother liked the driver in the Masai Mara	
6 Reason why Masai music is unusual	
7 **Two** reasons why Jamie wants to go to Kenya again	1 ______ 2 ______

c) *Would you like to go to Kenya on holiday? Write three or four sentences and explain why, or why not using examples from Jamie's text.* ____/ 5

6 READING Chapter 31

This text is a chapter from Mark Haddon's novel "The Curious Incident of the Dog in the Night-Time". Christopher Boone is fifteen years old and is autistic, a disability which means he is different to other children. The book opens with Christopher discovering his neighbour's dog dead. The dog has been killed. The police are called and they ask Christopher some questions. Christopher is upset by the situation and when one of the police officers tries to touch him, he hits him. The police arrest Christopher and take him to the police station. You are going to read about what happens when Christopher's father arrives.

It was 1:12 when Father arrived at the police station. I did not see him until 1:28 am but I knew he was there because I could hear him.

He was shouting, 'I want to see my son' and 'Why the hell is he locked up?' and 'Of course I'm bloody angry.'

Then I heard a policeman telling him to calm down. Then I heard nothing for a long while.

At 1:28 am a policeman opened the door of the cell and told me that there was someone to see me.

I stepped outside. Father was standing in the corridor. He held up his right hand and spread his fingers out in a fan. I held up my left hand and spread my fingers out in a fan and we made our fingers and thumbs touch each other. We do this because sometimes Father wants to give me a hug, but I do not like hugging people, so we do this instead, and it means that he loves me.

Then the policeman told us to follow him down the corridor to another room. In the room was a table and three chairs. He told us to sit down on the far side of the table and he sat down on the other side. There was a tape recorder on the table and I asked whether I was going to be interviewed and he was going to record the interview.

He said, 'I don't think there will be any need for that.' He was an inspector. I could tell because he wasn't wearing a uniform. He also had a very hairy nose. It looked as if there were two very small mice hiding in his nostrils[1].

He said, 'I have spoken to your father and he says that you didn't mean to hit the policeman.'

I didn't say anything because this wasn't a question.

He said, 'Did you mean to hit the policeman?'

I said, 'Yes.'

He squeezed his face and said, 'But you didn't mean to hurt the policeman?'

I thought about this and said, 'No. I didn't mean to hurt the policeman. I just wanted him to stop touching me.'

Then he said, 'You know that it is wrong to hit a policeman, don't you?'

I said, 'I do.'

He was quiet for a few seconds, then he asked, 'Did you kill the dog, Christopher?'

I said, 'I didn't kill the dog.'

He said, 'Do you know that it is wrong to lie to a policeman and that you can get into a very great deal of trouble if you do?'

---

[1]nostril *Nasenloch*

I said, 'Yes.'

He said, 'So, do you know who killed the dog?'

I said, 'No.'

He said, 'Are you telling the truth?'

I said, 'Yes. I always tell the truth.'

And he said, 'Right. I am going to give you a caution[1].'

I asked, 'Is that going to be on a piece of paper like a certificate I can keep?'

He replied, 'No, a caution means that we are going to keep a record of what you did, that you hit a policeman but that it was an accident and that you didn't mean to hurt the policeman.'

I said, 'But it wasn't an accident.'

And Father said, 'Christopher, please.'

The policeman closed his mouth and breathed out loudly through his nose and said, 'If you get into any more trouble, we will take out this record and see that you have been given a caution and we will take things much more seriously. Do you understand what I'm saying?'

I said I understood.

Then he said that we could go and he stood up and opened the door and we walked out into the corridor and back to the front desk where I picked up my Swiss Army Knife and my piece of string and the piece of the wooden puzzle and the 3 pellets of rat food for Toby and my £1.47 and the paperclip and my front door key which were all in a little plastic bag and we went out to Father's car which was parked outside and we drove home.

a) *What happens in the text? Put the sentences in the right order.* _____/ 8

_____ **A** Christopher's father was angry with the police officer.

_____ **B** He asked Christopher some questions.

_____ **C** Christopher could hear his father before he saw him at the police station.

_____ **D** The police gave Christopher back his things, and then he went home with his father.

_____ **E** When they saw each other, instead of a hug Christopher and his father made their fingers and thumbs touch each other.

_____ **F** Christopher answered the inspector's questions and told him that he did not kill the dog.

_____ **G** The police officer took them to a room with a table and three chairs.

_____ **H** Christopher was given a caution.

b) *In the introduction to the text you are told that Christopher is autistic, a disability which means he is different to other children. There are clues in the text to Christopher's autism. Find three of them.* _____/ 3

---

[1]caution *Verwarnung*

7 WRITING The story behind the picture

_____/ 20

Tell the story behind the picture in about 150 words. Use your imagination.

The questions below will help you:

- Who is the woman?
- What is behind the door?
- How does she feel? What has happened before?
- What will she do next?

8 WRITING Selling something on the internet

_____/ 20

Being a very clever and creative teenager, you invent gadgets (= products with a special function) in your free time. These gadgets help people master their everyday lives or special situations. You have invented the gadget in the picture.

Before you start writing, collect some ideas about what the gadget can be used for and what its special function is. Then create an advert for a website where you want to sell your gadget.

In this text include

- a catchy slogan/name for your product,
- a description of all the (special) functions it has,
- its price,
- information on postage and packing.

Write about 150 words. Use your imagination in this task!

9 MEDIATION Job advert

_____/ 11

Du bist interessiert an dem Job aus der Anzeige unten, weil du die Chance siehst, deine Ferien im Ausland zu verbringen. Deine Eltern möchten einige Dinge über diesen Job wissen.

Erkläre ihnen auf Deutsch:

- wo du arbeiten könntest, (2)
- welche Aufgaben du dort hättest, (1)
- welche Voraussetzungen du erfüllen musst und welche Erfahrungen du haben musst, (5)
- wann und wie lange du dort arbeiten müsstest, (2)
- wo du wohnen könntest. (1)

Employer: Lakeside Day Camp

Salary: None specified

Location: Dublin, Ireland

Description: Are you a student looking for summer work? Tired of the usual retail or bar job? How about working in childcare? ***Camp Lakeside*** can offer you a fun *summer job* that will boost your CV. You should have some experience working with children aged between 7 and 10 and the ability to create games and summer activities. This role is very active and based outdoors for much of the day. We need caring, energetic and enthusiastic people. If this is you, please apply and spend your summer learning while you earn! You must be at least 16 years old.

Seasonal contract from June until August. Minimum of nine weeks required. We offer accommodation on the site.

10 MEDIATION Das filmende Klassenzimmer

_____ / 12

There is a student from America in your class and he goes with you on a class trip to Munich.
One day you are going to visit the Bavaria Filmstadt, and he wants to know what you are going to do there.
You found the following information on the internet. It's in German.

Tell him in English what you are going to see and do.

DAS FILMENDE KLASSENZIMMER – DER STUNDENPLAN	
Ab 9.00 Uhr	Gruppenarbeit: Zuerst werden die Story gefunden, die Dialoge erarbeitet und die Rollen verteilt.
Ab ca. 10.30 Uhr	Klamotten und alle anderen Dinge, die man braucht, aussuchen.
Ab ca. 11.00 Uhr	Drehbeginn – an verschiedenen Locations der Bavaria Filmstadt, vor berühmten Gebäuden oder im Studio.
Ab ca. 14.00 Uhr am frühen Nachmittag	Drehschluss – jetzt geht's zur Exkursion in die Bavaria Filmstadt. Bei der Führung erfahrt ihr Spannendes aus der Welt von Kino & TV! Außerdem gibt es eine Stuntshow und ihr lernt die Geheimnisse des Filmemachens kennen.
In der Zwischenzeit	Profis der Bavaria machen ihre Hausaufgaben: bearbeiten euren Film
Ab ca. 16.30 Uhr	Die große Filmpremiere! Danach könnt ihr den fertigen Film auf DVD mit nach Hause nehmen.

Source: *http://www.germanplaces.com/de/freizeitparks-muenchen/freizeitpark-filmstadt-bavaria.html*
und: *http://www.filmstadt.de/fileadmin/bav_filmstadt/downloads/PDF_KLAZI_09.pdf*

11 WORDS My first job

_____ / 10

You will finish school next summer and at school you have learned how to apply for a job.

Read the following sentences and choose the right word to complete them.

First think about your interests and abilities. Then check the internet and find some company websites. Decide which company you should ***ask / apply*** to. After that write a letter of motivation and tell them why you are ***reading / writing*** and give some information about your ***qualifications / quantities***. At the end ask them for some information about their ***community / company*** and say you look forward to hearing from them soon.

Maybe you will get an ***invitation / invention*** to an interview! Then you send them an e-mail and ***accept / expect*** it. You can also ask them for information about public ***traffic / transport*** or car parking facilities.

For the interview you should dress ***strongly / suitably***. During the interview you should be polite and ***friendly / happy***. At the end they will let you know when they will ***contact / context*** you to tell you if you have got the job.

12 WORDS What is it?

a) *Which words are described here?* _____ / 5

1 Gas, smoke, etc. that factories release into the atmosphere: ______________________

2 A useful machine, e. g. a dishwasher, that makes the housework easier: ______________________

3 Electricity is produced there: ______________________

4 (to) say what you think: ______________________

5 Being poor: ______________________

b) *Describe what the words mean.* _____ / 10

1 (to) dump sb.: ______________________

2 appearance: ______________________

3 (to) be able to afford sth.: ______________________

4 (to) complain to sb. about sth.: ______________________

5 kettle: ______________________

13 WORDS Say it in English

____/ 18

Was sagst du, wenn …

1 … du einen Namen nicht verstanden hast? ______________________________

____

2 … du gerade einen Ferienjob angefangen hast? ______________________________

____

3 … deine Schwester im 6. Monat schwanger ist? ______________________________

____

4 … du etwas richtig gemein findest? ______________________________

____

5 … du deinen CO_2-Fußabdruck verringern willst? ______________________________

____

6 … deine Eltern dir nie erlauben, ins Ausland zu reisen? ______________________________

____

7 … deine Freunde dich nicht ernst nehmen? ______________________________

____

8 … du kurz mal mit jemandem reden möchtest? ______________________________

____

9 … es nicht deine Absicht war, jemanden zu unterbrechen? ______________________________

____

14 GRAMMAR At lunch break

_____ / 14

*Look at the picture and complete the text with the correct form of the verbs. Use the **simple present** or the **present progressive**.*

1 These students ____________________ (be) at school. They ____________________ (have) their lunch break.

2 The boy who ____________________ (use) his phone is Bob. On his right you can see Melissa. She ____________________ (send) a text message to her boyfriend.

3 She ____________________ (not talk) to the others because she ____________________ (think) they are boring.

4 The girl on the left ____________________ (be) Sophie. She usually ____________________ (wear) a hat, but in this picture she ____________________ (not wear) it. I ____________________ (not know) why.

5 The girl and the boy in the background ____________________ (come) from Germany. They ____________________ (spend) a year at our school to improve their English. I ____________________ (like) the boy very much.

6 Oh, and I ____________________ (be) in the picture too – the girl with the curly hair.

15 GRAMMAR Technology has changed our lives

_____ / 14

Choose the correct tense and underline the verb.

When I was a small child, lots of things ***are / were*** different. My parents ***don't have / didn't have*** a TV, so we ***listen / listened*** to the news on the radio. Now everybody ***has / had*** a TV in his room and can watch the programme he or she ***likes / liked***. But that also ***means / meant*** that we ***don't sit / didn't sit*** together in the living room any longer.

We ***go / went*** on holiday by train or by car. Today I ***flew / fly*** when I go abroad.

And computers! I ***send / sent*** lots of e-mails every day and ***get / got*** the answers the same day.

My father ***writes / wrote*** letters and ***has to / had to*** wait for the answers for days or even weeks.

So lots of things have changed. But, in my opinion, not everything ***is / was*** better today.

16 GRAMMAR Future plans

_____ / 6

Here are some personal statements from students who are leaving school next year.

Complete them with ***will*** *or* ***won't****.*

Bob	I hope my parents _______________ help me to find a good job. That's important for my career.
Jack	I don't know if I _______________ stay at home after I finish school.
Susan	My parents _______________ give me any pocket money after I have finished school.
Emily	I have to find a job near my home, but that _______________ be easy because there aren't many companies.
Sophie and David	We plan to go to the USA for a year. Perhaps we _______________ be able to work as volunteers.
Diana	I don't know what to do after school! Maybe I _______________ go to college.

Oral Exams

Übersicht der Aufgaben

Seite	Aufgabe	Kurzbeschreibung	Kompetenz	Punkte
77	1 **Problems on holiday**	Mit Hilfe eines Cartoons über Probleme, die bei Reisen mit der Familie bzw. auf Klassenfahrten auftreten können, sprechen	Monologisches Sprechen (Passt zu Unit 1)	20
77	2 **A holiday discussion**	Mit Hilfe von Rollenkarten einen Dialog zwischen einem Kind und einem Elternteil, die gemeinsam auf Mallorca Urlaub machen und unterschiedliche Vorstellungen davon haben, gestalten	Dialogisches Sprechen (Passt zu Unit 1)	20
78	3 **Different holiday plans**	Aus einer Auswahl von Urlaubsfotos diejenigen aussuchen, die die bevorzugte und die am wenigsten beliebte Form des Reisens zeigen, und darüber sprechen	Monologisches Sprechen[1] (Passt zu Unit 1)	20
79	4 **How to book a tour**	Mit Hilfe von Rollenkarten und Impulsen einen Dialog zwischen einem deutschen Touristen und einem Angestellten des Touristenbüros in Bala, Wales, gestalten	Dialogisches Sprechen (Passt zu Unit 1)	20
80	5 **Inventions**	Fotos von Alltagsgegenständen beschreiben. Den Gegenstand, den man für die wichtigste Erfindung hält, und den, ohne den man leben könnte, benennen	Monologisches Sprechen[1] (Passt zu Unit 2)	20
80	6 **Important items**	Aus der Fotoauswahl zu Aufgabe 5 drei Gegenstände auswählen, die man auf eine einsame Alpenhütte mitnehmen würde	Dialogisches Sprechen (Passt zu Unit 2)	20
81	7 **The best "product"**	Aus drei Kategorien ein Produkt auswählen und bewerben	Monologisches Sprechen (Passt zu Unit 2)	20
82	8 **A street interview**	Mit Hilfe von Rollenkarten ein Interview über umweltschützendes Verhalten führen	Dialogisches Sprechen (Passt zu Unit 2)	20

[1] Diese Fotos in Farbe finden Sie als kostenloses Online-Angebot auf unserer Website **www.englishg.de** unter >Downloads<.

Seite	Aufgabe	Kurzbeschreibung	Kompetenz	Punkte
83	9 **Summer jobs**	Aus drei Stellenanzeigen für einen Ferienjob in England eine aussuchen und darüber sprechen	Monologisches Sprechen (Passt zu Unit 3)	20
84	10 **A job interview**	Mit Hilfe von Rollenkarten und der Stellenanzeigen zu Aufgabe 9 ein Bewerbungsgespräch führen	Dialogisches Sprechen (Passt zu Unit 3)	20
84	11 **Different kinds of teachers**	Mit Hilfe von zwei Bildern über unterschiedliche Lehrertypen sprechen	Monologisches Sprechen	20
85	12 **School life**	Zwei Konfliktsituationen zwischen einem Schüler und einem Lehrer in Rollenspielen darstellen	Dialogisches Sprechen	20
85	13 **Bringing up children**	Mit Hilfe eines Cartoons darüber sprechen, was ein Kind lernen sollte und welche Erziehungsfehler Eltern machen können	Monologisches Sprechen	20
86	14 **Parents and children**	Eine Konfliktsituation zwischen einem Kind und einem Elternteil im Rollenspiel darstellen	Dialogisches Sprechen	20
87	15 **Casting shows**	Mit Hilfe eines Fotos und Impulsen über Casting Shows sprechen	Monologisches Sprechen	20
87	16 **How to become a star**	Einen Dialog über die Teilnahme an einer Casting Show führen	Dialogisches Sprechen	20
88	17 **At the airport**	Ein Bild einer Abflughalle eines Flughafens beschreiben	Monologisches Sprechen	20
88	18 **Lost luggage**	Einen Dialog zwischen einem Passagier und einem Flughafen-angestellten über einen verlorenen Koffer führen	Dialogisches Sprechen	20
89	19 **Facebook**	Der Großmutter Facebook beschreiben	Monologisches Sprechen	20
89	20 **Pros and cons of Facebook**	Einen Dialog über die Vor- und Nachteile von Facebook führen	Dialogisches Sprechen	20

1 SPEAKING Problems on holiday

_____ / 20

Describe the picture.

What's the message of the cartoon?

What kind of problems can you have (after a few days) when you spend your holidays with your family?

Can you give a "real" example of an argument you had during your holidays or on a class trip?

How did you solve the problem?

Speak for about five minutes. You've got three minutes to prepare your talk.

"I'd like to spend the holidays with my loved ones, but after the third day, they're not loved ones anymore!"

2 SPEAKING A holiday discussion

_____ / 20

Imagine you and your mother/father are spending your summer holiday on Majorca right now. After three days there are some problems.

Prepare and act out a dialogue of about five minutes. You've got five minutes to prepare it.

Partner A

You are the son/daughter.
You spent the last three days on the beach, lying in the sun, sleeping or doing watersports.
At night you had fun in the hotel disco and went to bed early in the morning.
That's all you want to do during your stay here.
But your mother's/father's plans are different.

Start a discussion with her/him and try to find a solution or compromise.

Partner B

You are the father/mother.
You spent the last three days on the beach which was OK, but now you want to see something of this beautiful island. You want to do some sightseeing and rent a car, for example, or visit the capital.
But your son/daughter always wants to go to the beach.

Start a discussion and try to find a solution or compromise.

3 SPEAKING Different holiday plans

_____/ 20

Look at the photos and the task. Do not write anything down. Start talking when you're ready.
Say what the photos show.

Choose the photo that shows your favourite kind of holiday and describe what you would do there.
Why is it your favourite?

Then choose the photo which shows the kind of holiday you wouldn't like at all and say why.
Which was your best/worst holiday or class trip ever and why?

4 SPEAKING How to book a tour

___ / 20

This year, you and your family are spending the summer holidays in Wales. You have decided to go on a river rafting tour together and, because you are the only one in your family who speaks English, you book the tour at the tourist information in Bala.

Act out the situation in a role play. Use the role cards. You can add more information if you like. Prepare and act out a dialogue of about five minutes. You've got three minutes to prepare your talk.

Partner A

You are the son/daughter and book the tour.

Here are your facts:

- *You want to join the tour on August 3rd (there are three of you)*
- *Ask when the tour starts*
- *Ask about the costs*
- *Ask what special things you have to bring with you*
- *...*
- *You want to pay by credit card*
- *You decide to book the tour and finish the conversation in a polite way*

Partner B

You are the man/woman who works at the tourist information in Bala and you help the tourist to book the river rafting tour.

Here are your facts:

- *You have got 10 seats left on the tour*
- *The tour starts at 10.00 am at the river*
- *Price: £43 per person*
- *Things to know:*
  - *No alcohol before or during the tour*
  - *No non-swimmers*
  - *No cameras (water!), no jewellery*
  - *People must be at least 1.20 m tall*
- *Things people have to bring with them:*
  - *Trainers, towels, swimwear, warm tops*
  - *Something to eat and drink*
- *People will get:*
  - *Helmets, paddles; wetsuits can be hired*
- *Paying by credit card or cash possible*
- *Book the tour and then finish the conversation in a polite way*

5 SPEAKING Inventions

_____/ 20

Look at the photos and say what they show.
Which of these gadgets do you think is the most useful and why?
Choose one gadget you could live without and give reasons why.
Talk for about five minutes. You've got three minutes to prepare your talk.

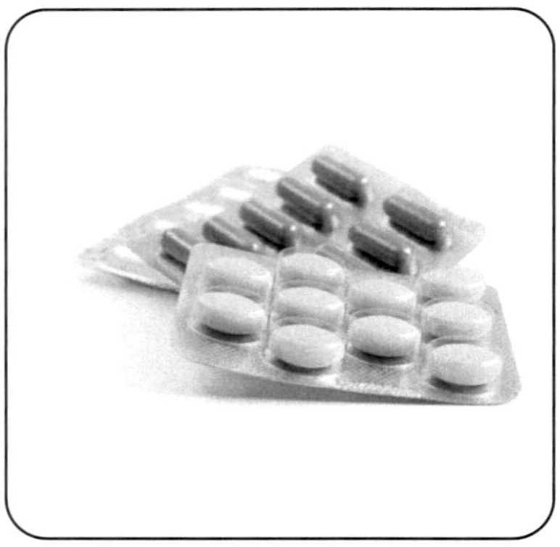

6 SPEAKING Important items[1]

_____/ 20

Imagine you and your friend are going to take part in a new TV reality show where you will stay in an alpine hut in the Swiss Alps for two months.
A camera team will accompany you. The director has agreed to let you take three gadgets with you.
Start a discussion and decide on which three things you couldn't live without. You can choose items from the photos or you can add your own ideas.
Don't forget to give good reasons for your choice.
Prepare and act out a dialogue of about five minutes. You've got five minutes to prepare your talk.

---

[1] Für diese Aufgabe müssen die Schüler/innen dieselben Fotos wie für Aufgabe 5 erhalten.

7 SPEAKING The best "product"

_____ / 20

1. Sports equipment

For example: a new racket/ball/board/T-shirt/shorts/shoes/helmet/bike/skateboard, etc.
Think about new technology (faster, better, waterproof, lightweight, easier to handle, …)

2. Free time activities

For example: big events that will take place (in your town) soon: concerts (think of possible bands/groups/stars), other events (sports events, musicals, comedy shows, festivals, …)

3. Technical equipment

For example: mobile phones, computers or game consoles, …
Think about new technology (the latest, fastest, best, greatest, …) and explain why people must have this gadget.

Look at the descriptions. Imagine you are a salesperson and your job is to choose ***one*** *of these things. Choose the one which you think is the most useful. You have got three minutes to prepare an interesting talk on it.*

Don't forget to give as many reasons as possible explaining why people should buy it.

Your aim is to sell as many of your chosen "product" as possible, so try to convince your listeners in about three minutes.

8 SPEAKING A street interview

_____ / 20

One of you is a teenager who has to interview adults for your school magazine. The topic is the environment. You've got five minutes to prepare the interview which should last for about five minutes.

Partner A

You are a boy/girl who has to write an article for your school magazine. You are interviewing an adult about the environment.

- *Start the conversation in a friendly way and ask if you can interview him/her*
- *Tell him/her the topic*
- *Ask about the technology he/she uses in daily life and why*
- *Ask if he/she does anything special to save the environment (If not, give examples of what he/she could do.)*
- *Ask what he/she uses fresh water for and give examples of how to use less water*
- *Ask which gadget he/she could live without for one week, and which he/she couldn't be without at all and why*
- *Tell him/her about an environment project you're doing at your school (for example: avoiding waste, using less electricity) and ask him/her if he/she would like to join in*
- *Ask for permission to take a photo of him/her and to print the interview in the next edition of the school magazine*
- *Thank him/her for the interview and say goodbye*

Partner B

You are a man/woman walking through your town. A boy/girl asks you for an interview.

- *You have got time for the interview if it doesn't take too long*
- *You want to know what it will be about*
- *Tell him/her the gadgets/technology you use in daily life and what you use them for (think of things in the bathroom, kitchen, etc.)*
- *Tell him/her that you don't do anything special for the environment and you don't know what you could do. Ask for examples*
- *Tell him/her that you think you use too much water every day and give examples*
- *Be prepared to be asked which gadget you could live without for one week and which one you couldn't*
- *Ask him/her if his/her school does anything special for the environment*
- *Say if you would be interested in taking part in the "school project" or not and why*
- *Allow him/her to print the interview but refuse the photo*
- *Say goodbye*

9 SPEAKING Summer jobs

_____/ 20

You are looking for a summer job and you have found three adverts on www.summerjobs.co.uk.

- *Say which job you think is the best and which one is the worst.*
  Give reasons for your choice.
- *Decide which job you would like to do and why you think you would be the right person for the job.*
  Talk for about three minutes. You've got five minutes to prepare your talk.

Au pair in Edinburgh, Scotland

We are looking for an au pair boy or girl from Europe.
We (Maggie, 39 and Steven, 40) have got three children (our twins Ben and Jack are 3 years old and our daughter Lily is 6 years old).
If you love children, you are the person we are looking for! You will have to look after our children while we are at work, assist us in the household and go on holiday with us to the beautiful Highlands. You will be able to improve your English, and we will welcome you as a new member of our family.

If you are interested, please contact
the Au pair & Nanny Agency in London, Mrs Riley,
tel.: 0044-1288 359159

Children's Hospital, Bloomsbury, London

Positive-thinking teenager required who loves to entertain sick children.

- Working hours from 11 am–6 pm
- £3.64 per hour
- From July–September
- Minimum age: 15
- Experience an advantage

Please contact Mr Smith, tel.: 0044-020 7405 9200

Funpark, Adventure Island, England
Summer work

Age: 15–20 years

Jobs: various rides, like the roller coaster, etc., restaurants (prepare and sell food/drinks)

You should be a polite and friendly person.

Months: June–October

Please contact
Judy Miller, tel.: 0044-01702443004

10 SPEAKING A job interview[1] ____ / 20

Read the job descriptions carefully and agree on an advert.
Then one of you applies for this job. Act out the job interview.
Use the role cards.
You've got ten minutes to prepare an interview of about five minutes.

Partner A

- *You are the applicant*
- *You really want to get the job*
- *Talk about your personal qualities, your interests, …*
- *Be prepared to answer some questions about yourself and your interest in the job*
- *Ask when the job starts*
- *Ask about the pay*
- *Be friendly and polite*

Partner B

- *You are interviewing partner A for the job*
- *Welcome him/her and be friendly*
- *Ask about his/her personal qualities, interests, why he/she is interested in the job, and other things you would like to know*
- *Be prepared to answer some questions about the advert and the pay, working hours, customers, …*
- *Thank him/her and tell him/her you will be in touch and say goodbye*

11 SPEAKING Different kinds of teachers ____ / 20

Look at the two pictures and describe which person you would prefer as your form teacher and why.
Imagine one lesson with him and describe it.
Start talking when you're ready.

---

[1] Für diese Aufgabe müssen die Schüler/innen dieselben Stellenanzeigen wie für Aufgabe 9 erhalten.

12 SPEAKING School life

_____ / 20

Imagine one of you is a student and the other one a form teacher at school and you are having a conversation.

Partner A

Imagine you are the student.

The lesson has already started, but you arrive 10 minutes late and you haven't done your homework either.

Think of a good apology and good reasons for being late and for not doing your homework.

Suggest possible solutions.

Now swap roles and act out a situation where the teacher has found out that two students have copied from each other during a test.

This time you are the teacher.

Partner B

You are the teacher and right now your lesson is being interrupted by a pupil who is late.

You also discover that he/she hasn't done the homework.

How will you react and what will you say?

Now swap roles and act out a situation where the teacher has found out that two students have copied from each other during a test.

You are one of the students.

13 SPEAKING Bringing up children

_____ / 20

"I think he's ready to start using the computer. He just said 'Google'!"

Describe the picture.

What's the message of the cartoon?

Describe the "perfect child".

What do you think a child should really learn during the first five years of his/her life?

Tell us about the biggest mistakes that parents could make when they are raising a child.

Look at the cartoon and the task. Do not write anything down. Start talking when you're ready.

14 SPEAKING Parents and children

_____ / 20

Parents and children often have a different point of view on many topics.
These topics could be: drinking alcohol, going out, coming home at a certain time, parties, friends, piercings, computer games, school/job, etc.

Decide on one of the topics on the role cards or on one mentioned above to start a discussion. You've got ten minutes to prepare a discussion of five minutes.

Partner A

You are the son/daughter.

- *You want your own TV in your room and to be allowed to watch TV whenever you want to.*

Or

- *You want the latest mobile phone.*

Or

- *You want to start taking driving lessons and expect your parents to pay for them.*

Or

- *You are fed up using your father's/mother's computer. You want your own and free internet access.*

Or

- *You hate having to come home from parties at midnight. You want to be allowed to stay out as long as you want to.*

- *Say exactly what you want or don't want and why.*
- *Give good reasons for your statements.*
- *Think of possible ways to convince your father/mother that you are right.*
- *What could you do or say to show your father/mother that you are willing to find a solution or compromise? What have you got to offer?*
  Try to be diplomatic.

Partner B

You are the father/mother. Your child complains about several things.

- *Your child wants his/her own TV in his/her room and to be allowed to watch TV whenever he/she wants to.*

Or

- *Your child wants the latest mobile phone.*

Or

- *Your child wants to start taking driving lessons and expects you to pay for them.*

Or

- *Your child is fed up using your computer. He/She wants his/her own and free internet access.*

Or

- *Your child hates having to come home from parties at midnight. He/She wants to be allowed to stay out as long as he/she wants to.*

- *Listen carefully to him/her and be polite and calm.*
- *Tell him/her your opinion and explain why you think this way.*
- *Think of possible ways to convince your son/daughter that you are right.*
- *What could you do or say to show your child that you are willing to find a solution or compromise? What have you got to offer?*
  Try to be diplomatic.

15 SPEAKING Casting shows

_____ / 20

- *Describe the photo/scene.*
- *What are the people in the photo doing?*
- *Do you watch casting shows? Why? / Why not? / What do/don't you like about them?*
- *Casting shows are also called "talent shows". What kind of talents are people looking for?*
- *Could you imagine applying to take part in a casting show? Why? / Why not?*
- *How do you think the life of the winner changes? Or does it not change at all?*
- *Are there any possible dangers?*

Start talking when you are ready.

16 SPEAKING How to become a star

_____ / 20

Work out a dialogue between two friends. One of you wants to apply to take part in a casting show, because you think you have got a special talent (and dream of becoming a star, getting rich and having a fantastic future).

The other one

a) *thinks that this is a good idea and together you plan further steps (but don't forget to warn your friend of possible dangers).*

or

b) *doesn't think that this is a good idea and tries to convince the other person of his/her opinion.*

You've got three minutes to prepare a dialogue of about five minutes.

17 SPEAKING At the airport

_____/ 20

Talk about the picture. Think about the people, the things, the police officers and a possible story.

18 SPEAKING Lost luggage

_____/ 20

Imagine you have flown to New York and when you arrive, your suitcase is missing.

You go to your airline's baggage service and ask for help. Prepare a role play of about five minutes using the role cards below. You have got three minutes to prepare it.

Partner A

You are the tourist whose luggage is missing.

- *Tell the person at the baggage service desk where you have come from and what exactly is missing*
- *Describe your suitcase: colour, size, anything special (inside), it has a label with your name*
- *Tell him/her your home address and your address in New York and how long you are staying there*
- *Ask when the suitcase will be returned*
- *Tell him/her how you feel about the situation*

Partner B

You work at an airline's baggage service desk. A tourist comes to you and tells you that he/she has lost his/her luggage.

- *Be friendly and polite and apologize*
- *Try to calm him/her down*
- *Ask:*
  - *for his/her departure airport*
  - *what exactly he/she has lost*
  - *for his/her full name (spelling), home and holiday address*
  - *when he/she is flying home again*
- *Tell him/her when the suitcase might be returned (1–3 days)*
- *Finish the conversation in a polite and friendly way*

19 SPEAKING Facebook

_____ / 20

Imagine you're having lunch together with your family and you're talking about "Facebook".

Your 70-year-old grandmother is listening to your conversation but doesn't understand a word of what you're saying. Try to explain in a few sentences what "Facebook" is, what you can/can't do with it and why you like/don't like to use it.

Now your grandmother is interested in using "Facebook" too. What advice would you give her?

20 SPEAKING Pros and cons of Facebook[1]

_____ / 20

Imagine you met a new friend on holiday. At the end of the holiday you suggest keeping in touch via Facebook. Unfortunately your new friend doesn't use Facebook.

You want to find out his/her reasons. Start a conversation. Use the information below and add your own ideas if you can. You can start your conversation with a question. For example: "Tell me, why don't you use …?"

You've got five minutes to prepare a conversation of five minutes.

Partner A (pros)

- *free-time activity / not bored any more*
- *play games*
- *chat with your friends / see when they are online or offline / read what they are doing*
- *make new friends / belong to a group*
- *"outsider" if you don't use it*
- *Facebook faster than e-mails / don't need friends' e-mail addresses / uncomplicated*
- *Facebook – connected to the web. Things can be read worldwide*
- *parents can't look at private things if you don't let them*

Partner B (cons)

- *waste of time / can do better things instead*
- *don't want to read boring things about other people*
- *"dangerous publishing" / strangers can look at private photos and store them on their PC*
- *you give away private details / low protection / people can see when you're on/offline*
- *many Facebook "friends" – not real friends / better to meet them in reality or phone them*
- *careless users publish private details not only on Facebook but also on the internet / details can appear everywhere!*
- *your future boss can find embarrassing photos of you / bad for job applications*
- *parents can log in too / check up on their children (what they say, do, where they are/no privacy for children)*

[1] Hinweis für die Lehrkraft: Für leistungsstärkere Schüler/innen können Ideen auf den Rollenkarten entfernt werden

Unit 1 Love life!

p. 8/9 **1 Small talk**

a) *1* c *2* a *3* c

b) *1* Brighton
2 on holiday / wants to see many cities
3 (from) Hamburg
4 (somewhere) near Brighton
5 go to a café (in the Lanes) / drink/buy smoothie / sit on the beach / swim in the sea / go to the pier / go to a fun fair / play games there / enjoy the fresh air

c) Part 1:
1 Glasgow
2 storms in the London area
3 3.30

Part 2:
1 a) (for) three weeks
b) work experience in Glasgow / going to work for a film company / going to help the director to organize a (historical) film in Scotland
2 lives there / beautiful island / off the West Coast / many animals / deer, eagles, sea birds
3 having a coffee together / going to a café

p. 10 **2 My favourite films**

1 action / horror / science fiction films / cartoons / comedies (drei davon = 1 P)
2 romantic comedies / sentimental films
3 special effects / (great) actors / (great) story / James Cameron = favourite director
4 a) twice a month
b) special effects / (bigger) screen / can watch films in 3D / better sound
5 a comedy / set in Britain / about a group of teenagers (growing up) / got it for his dad
6 they are not always right / can be wrong / prefers reaction from friends
7 a) on Saturday b) *Twilight Saga* c) with friends

p. 11 **3 Depressed**

Individuelle Lösung

p. 12 **4 In the school canteen**

Individuelle Lösung

p. 13–15 **5 A famous film director and a famous film**

Text I
1 he only enjoyed Art lessons (at school)
2 over 2,500
3 *The Duellists*
4 *Blade Runner*
5 *Gladiator*
6 Russell Crowe

Text II
True: 3, 5, 8
False: 1, 6, 7
Not given: 2, 4

6 Tears of a clown p. 16/17

a) Arnold: E; Dawn: A; Rowdy: D

b) Arnold: lovesick, unhappy
Dawn: beautiful, cool
Rowdy: rude, tough
passen nicht: lazy, thin

c) *1* Arnold; She would never become his girlfriend because she thought she was better than him.
2 Arnold; He was making fun of him. / He only pretended to be asleep.
3 Arnold; I want to tell you something that is very important to me.
4 Rowdy; Dawn doesn't care about you. / Dawn isn't interested in you.
5 Arnold; It's very weak.
6 Rowdy; Stop crying.

7 What should a real friend be like? p. 18

Individuelle Lösung

8 Lots of problems p. 18

Individuelle Lösung

9 A film I've watched p. 18

Individuelle Lösung

10 What is this film about? p. 19

Main characters:
Ben: disabled, sits in a wheelchair, needs help, but bullies his mum and other people who take care of him
Christian: is studying medicine, Ben's social worker, is funny
Annika: music student, has to decide between Ben and Christian
Plot:
Ben's new social worker Christian gets along well with him, they become friends
Ben and Christian both fall in love with Annika;
first Annika is attracted by Christian, a happy boy;
Ben thinks he hasn't got a chance with Annika because he's in a wheelchair.
But things are different. Finally, Annika dates Ben and their relationship develops.
General comment:
A film about friendship, love, sexuality and disability with a sense of humour
The characters' funny dialogues in a difficult relationship make the film special.

p. 19 **11 I've got mail**

Erics Situation:
- Hausarrest, da er im Zeugnis ein F in Mathe hat
- darf nicht zu Besuch nach Deutschland kommen

Wie Eric die Situation sieht:
- (hatte schon immer Probleme in Mathe)
- hat oft seine Hausaufgaben mit Alex, dem Matheass, gemacht.
- bat Mathelehrer um Hilfe, der aber ablehnte
- wird Mathe nacharbeiten, sobald er aus Deutschland zurück ist

Erics Eltern:
- denken, er hat nicht ausreichend für Mathe gearbeitet
- sagen, er hat zu viel mit seinen Freunden herumgehangen
- glauben nicht, dass er sich mit Alex wegen Mathe getroffen hat
- wollen, dass er das Schuljahr wiederholt
- sagen, er soll im Sommer einen Mathekurs belegen

(– erlauben ihm nicht, den Freund in Deutschland zu besuchen)

p. 20 **12 What a person can be or look like**

a) *1* arrogant
2 unattractive
3 thin
4 lazy
5 fair/nice
6 straight

b) *1* lovable
2 attractive/good-looking
3 intelligent

c) Individuelle Lösung

p. 20 **13 Choose the right verb**

1 b *2* a *3* b *4* d

p. 21 **14 Find the right words**

a) *1* reviewer
2 (to) bite
3 (to) recommend
4 pregnant
5 patient
6 special effects

b) Mögliche Lösung:
1 the world around us
2 a special prize given to people who have done something well
3 a person who gives instructions to the actors, camera team, etc.
4 an article in a magazine or newspaper about a film or book

c) exam: take, pass, fail, sit, finish, do well/badly in an exam
film: watch, direct, record, make, rent a film

15 Family photo p. 22

a) Mögliche Lösung:
1 Mr Carter is (sitting in a chair) reading a newspaper.
2 The children are watching TV.
3 The children are sitting on the floor / in front of the sofa.
4 The girls are sitting next to each other.
5 The boy is lying in front of his sisters.
6 Mrs Carter is still at work / out doing the shopping / in the kitchen preparing dinner.

b) *1* We usually spend the evenings together in the living room.
2 I read the newspaper every evening.
3 I don't read the newspaper in the morning because I always leave the house at 5 am.
4 I sometimes watch TV with my brother and sister.
5 I go to the cinema with some/my friends once a month.
6 We usually go on Monday evening because there's a special ticket price.

c) Individuelle Lösung

Unit 2 The world we live in

p. 25/26 **1 London's new bike hire scheme**

a) **Text 1**

A7 B5 C4 D8 E6 F2 G1 H3

b) **Text 2**

1 cheaper than bus / visit city without stress / car drivers polite / help tourists
2 some cars are too fast / don't know the streets at all / traffic is on the wrong side / lose orientation / bikes are too heavy / too big for Spanish women

c) **Text 3**

1 they're dark blue / with a (Transport for London) logo on them
2 online
3 a cycle key
4 any of the (6000) bikes in the city
5 pay by credit card (at the docking station)
6 the first half hour is free
7 repair the bikes
8 a greener (and cycle-friendly) city

p. 27/28 **2 An audio guide**

a) *1* 1940s
2 early 1980s
3 in cars
4 1990s
5 between 100 and 200 g/grams/grammes
6 a) UK; b) 1992
7 mid 2000s
8 a) make telephone calls / check e-mails
b) instant messaging
9 a) faster and better on the internet
b) make video calls

b) *1* c *2* a *3* d *4* c *5* b *6* a

p. 29 **3 It's hot today, isn't it?**

Individuelle Lösung

p. 29 **4 Holiday plans**

Individuelle Lösung

p. 30–32 **5 Welcome to a year without garbage**

a) *1* c *2* c *3* b *4* a *5* b *6* c

b) Mögliche Lösung:
1 1 Nephews are visiting in the summer
2 Christmas
3 Eating out
4 Grocery shopping
5 Travelling
2 16,000
3 32%
4 1 buy local, organic, cruelty-free, fair-trade products
2 buy biodegradable cleaning products
3 recycle
4 use green bags to carry purchases
5 more than 1,600 pounds

p. 33–35 **6 Teenagers and technology**

a) *True:* 1, 2, 7, 9, 10
False: 4, 6, 8
Not given: 3, 5

b) Mögliche Lösung
1 75%
2 1 text
2 take pictures / share pictures
3 listen to music
4 play games
5 swap videos
6 access social networking sites
3 about 30
4 1 cheaper than calls
2 can do it in classroom
3 boredom
5 1 after school
2 nine or ten in the evening
6 someone posted an ugly photo (and refused to take it down)

7 The importance of recycling p. 36

Individuelle Lösung

8 The Green Garbage Project p. 36

Individuelle Lösung

9 Stadtrad Hamburg p. 37

There are 70 docking stations all over Hamburg. One is at the main station. The bikes (you can hire) are red. (You pay by EC or credit card.) The first 30 minutes are free. After that you pay per minute. One minute costs between 4 and 8 cents.

To hire a bike you have to activate the touch screen at the docking station with your EC or credit card. Then you have to choose the number of bikes you want to hire. Then you get a code that you have to key into the displays of the bikes you want to hire. Returning the bike is easy too: you lock it at the docking station and press the button on the lock. Then you can see a receipt code, which you have to key into together with the bike number. Then you can see how much you have to pay.

10 How to reduce your carbon footprint p. 38

You Kauf Hefte aus Recyclingpapier – neues Papier herzustellen benötigt sehr viel Wasser.

You dreh den Wasserhahn zu, während du dir die Zähne putzt. Spül die Toilette seltener und benutze sie nicht als Abfalleimer. Dusch kürzer.

You Dreh das Licht ab, wenn du aus dem Zimmer gehst. Lass Geräte nicht im Standby-Modus. Schalte die Heizung runter.

You ich kann sie bitten, Sachen in Recyclingverpackungen zu kaufen und Geschenke in Zeitungspapier einzupacken.

You Nimm die Treppe statt des Fahrstuhls – das hält dich auch fit.

11 Saving the planet p. 39

1 a *2* b *3* c *4* a *5* b *6* a *7* c *8* c
9 a *10* c

12 Appliances you use every day p. 40

a) *1* remote (control)
2 light bulb
3 microwave
4 heating
5 charger

b) Individuelle Lösung

p. 40 **13 In the past and now**

a) wrote send produce didn't care listened use play went played didn't find used asked switch on

b) Mögliche Lösung:
In the past people used their telephone to phone people. Today they also use their phones to send text messages.
In the past people listened to the news on the radio. Today they watch the news on TV.
In the past people went on holiday by car. Today they go by plane.
In the past people read books. Today they listen to audiobooks.

Unit 3 Have your say!

p. 43 **1 Webcast: Stanley Park School**

1 build a new IT block
2 as a sports field
3 they practise twice a week at the moment; if field is sold, they will only be able to practise once a week / will have to share the other field with the football team
4 computer-based lessons / at lunch breaks and after school for homework / for group projects
5 comes from a large family / lives in small noisy house / shares computer with his brother and sisters
6 met with Mrs Andrews / organizing a petition / collecting signatures / had interview with local newspaper / thinking of organizing demonstrations outside school

p. 44 **2 The National Youth Rights Association**

1 Talk about their work and projects / Get more young people involved in their work
2 (Work to) support civil rights and freedoms for young people / Create a new world without discrimination
3 More than 10,000
4 Lowering voting age / Lowering drinking age / Protecting students' rights / Fighting ageism
5 Can be sent to adult prisons / Can become soldiers
6 Can't vote
7 Organize campaigns / Hand out flyers / Organize meetings and debates
8 Talk to Matt and Sarah / Look on the website / Download flyers

p. 45 **3 Young people and politics**

Individuelle Lösung

p. 46 **4 A discussion with your host family**

Individuelle Lösung

p. 47/48 **5 Award for teenager who nursed her dying friend**

a) *1* stayed up all night / looked after his medication / let him stay at her house / organized a party
2 last August / August 2009
3 cancer
4 let him spend Christmas with the family, gave him a stocking
5 at school / in the sixth form
6 the School Minister / Nick Gibb
7 Royal Marsden
8 in Sophie's house

b) individuelle Lösung

6 About the UK Youth Parliament p. 49/50

1 once a year / annually / every year
2 11–18
3 support campaigns, debate online
4 work experience, careers advisor
5 anti-bullying policy
6 cheaper fares for young people, easy access for disabled people
7 before 2020 / as soon as possible
8 1.7 million

7 Jane Goodall's Roots & Shoots p. 51/52

1 b *2* a *3* b *4* c *5* b *6* c *7* a *8* b

8 Young and old drivers p. 53

Individuelle Lösung

9 Teenage drinking p. 54

Individuelle Lösung

10 Travelling alone p. 54

Mögliche Lösung:
1 Das Kind soll die Adresse der nächsten Botschaft / des nächsten Konsulats kennen
2 Man soll eine Reiseversicherung mit entsprechender Deckung(ssumme) abschließen
3 Man soll einen guten Reiseführer kaufen, damit das Kind sich mit den Gesetzen und Gebräuchen des Reiselandes vertraut machen kann
4 Das Kind braucht einen gültigen Reisepass, und man soll Kopien davon machen
5 Eltern sollen dem Kind ausreichend Geld für die Reise und eine Reserve mitgeben

6 Das Kind muss wissen, wie es die Eltern kontaktieren kann, und die Eltern müssen wissen, wie sie das Kind erreichen können

p. 55 **11 Wahlen zum Jugendparlament**

Mögliche Lösung:

1 Things young people are interested in and things that are interesting for everybody (e. g. the environment)
2 No (you don't have to be a party member). Active members have to be between 13 and 18.
3 Young people between 12 and 18
4 In schools, during breaks, in free lessons and after school
5 Every two years / Every other year

p. 56 **12 Speak out!**

1 care about
2 take action
3 criticize
4 improve
5 makes sense
6 deserve

13 Explaining words p. 56

a) *1* town hall
2 equal
3 politician
4 moderator
5 prime minister

b) Mögliche Lösungen:
1 long part in a house, from which doors lead into rooms
2 money that the government gets from people's pay and from selling goods
3 an organization which politicians with the same political ideas belong to
4 (to) write your name on something with your hand
5 a request for something that a lot of people sign

14 A school project p. 57

for in in around from across in
with on for near in to to

15 Youth Conference p. 58

1 c *2* d *3* c *4* a *5* d *6* a *7* a *8* b

Exam File

p. 61 **1 Messages**

Text 1
1 a job interview
2 Monday or Tuesday (next week / the following week)
3 784682
4 if she's going to be in/home for tea tonight

Text 2
1 lots of traffic
2 a bad/nasty accident
3 there's no driver

Text 3
1 approximately 2 hours and 30 minutes
2 no
3 11.35
4 it's warm (28 degrees) and sunny

Text 4
1 4 pm, 8 pm, 10 pm
2 6 pm, 8.15 pm, -
3 3 pm, 5 pm, 7 pm

p. 62 **2 A job interview**

1 year 11; (Bathwick) High School
2 c
3 in the local newspaper
4 no
5 yes, helps her mother in the kitchen / did a food hygiene course at school
6 reliable / well-organized / gets good marks at school / helps in the library in lunch breaks
7 1 the salary; 2 how much money the guests leave behind; 3 working hours; 4 paid holidays

3 Future life p. 63

Individuelle Lösung

4 Solving problems abroad p. 64

Individuelle Lösung

5 Jamie's blog: On safari in Kenya p. 65/66

a) *True:* 2, 5, 8
False: 1, 4, 6
Not given: 3, 7

b) *1* his father's 50th birthday
2 1. elephants; 2. views of Mount Kilimanjaro
3 (to see) the sunrise (over Mountain Kilimanjaro)
4 They cover the lake. / their number
5 He was very funny and made her laugh.
6 They only use their voices. / They have/use no instruments.
7 1. Tourism is very important for Kenya.
2. He wants to see the beaches on the Indian Ocean.

c) Individuelle Lösung

p. 67/68 **6 Chapter 31**

a) 1 C 2 A 3 E 4 G 5 B 6 F 7 H 8 D

b) Mögliche Lösungen:

Christopher and his father don't hug, because he doesn't like being touched.

When the police officer starts talking to him, Christopher doesn't understand that he wants him to explain his actions.

He hit the policeman on purpose. / He says he hit the policeman on purpose.

He doesn't (seem to) understand what a caution is. / He thinks a caution is a good thing. / He doesn't understand why a caution is so important for him.

p. 69 **7 The story behind the picture**

Individuelle Lösung

p. 69 **8 Selling something on the internet**

Individuelle Lösung

p. 69 **9 Job advert**

Mögliche Lösung:

Ich könnte im Lakeside Day Camp in Dublin, Irland, arbeiten. Ich würde mit 7–10 Jahre alten Kindern den Tag verbringen, Spiele organisieren und viel draußen sein. Ich sollte Erfahrung mit Kindern dieses Alters haben und in der Lage sein, mir Spiele und Sommeraktivitäten auszudenken. Ich müsste zwischen Juni und August mindestens neun Wochen dort arbeiten. Ich könnte auf dem Gelände wohnen.

p. 70 **10 Das filmende Klassenzimmer**

Mögliche Lösung:

From 9 am till about 10.30 am we'll do group work. First we'll find the story, write the dialogues and say who is going to play which role.

At about 10.30 we'll choose clothes and other things we'll need (for our film).

At about 11 am we'll start filming at different locations in 'Bavaria Filmstadt', in front of famous buildings or in the studio.

At about 2 pm we'll finish filming and go on an excursion around 'Bavaria Filmstadt'. We'll hear some interesting things about the cinema and television. We'll watch a stunt show and learn about the secrets of film-making.

In the meantime people who work at 'Bavaria Filmstadt' will have cut our film.

At about 4.30 pm we're going to watch our film. After that we can take it home on DVD.

p. 71 **11 My first job**

apply writing qualifications company
invitation accept transport suitably friendly
contact

12 What is it? p. 71

a)
1 emission
2 appliance
3 power station
4 (to) speak out
5 poverty

b) Mögliche Lösungen:
1 (to) break up with sb.
2 what someone looks like
3 (to) have enough money to buy sth.
4 (to) tell sb. that you do not like sth.
5 a kitchen gadget that you use to heat water

13 Say it in English p. 72

Mögliche Lösungen:
1 (Excuse me,) could you repeat your name, please?
2 I've just started a holiday/summer job.
3 My sister is six months pregnant.
4 That's really mean.
5 I want to reduce my carbon footprint.
6 My parents never allow me to travel abroad.
7 My friends don't take me seriously.
8 Can I have a word with you?
9 Sorry, I didn't mean to interrupt you.

14 At lunch break p. 73
1 are are having
2 is using is sending
3 isn't talking thinks
4 is wears isn't wearing don't know
5 come are spending like
6 am / 'm

15 Technology has changed our lives p. 73

were didn't have listened has likes
means don't sit went fly send get
wrote had to is

16 Future plans p. 74

will will won't won't will will

Zu den Oral Exams werden keine Lösungsvorschläge gemacht.

Illustrationen

Katharina Wieker Berlin (S. 8; 22 unten; 29; 54; 69 unten; 73; 84; 88)

Bildquellen

Alamy, Abingdon (S. 63 oben re.: Pontino, unten li.: littlebloke; S. 78 Tower Bridge: Pawel Libera Images, unten li.: Cultura / Monty Rakusen; S. 79: Barrie Harwood);
cinetext, Frankfurt/Main (S. 19: Zorro Film);
Corbis, Düsseldorf (S. 65 oben: Tim Davis, 2. v. oben: William Manning);
Uschi Fleischhauer, Hannover (S. 78 unten re., unten Mitte);
Getty Images, München (S. 63 oben Mitte; S. 69 oben: Todd Warnock; S. 78 2. v. unten li.: R&D FOTO, 2. v. oben re.: Lisa Peardon; S. 87: Stockbyte (RF));
Gian Vaitl / www.sucht-info.ch (S. 22 oben);
Randy Glasbergen /glasbergen.com (S. 77; S. 85);
iStockphoto, Calgary (S. 36: MHJ; S. 65 unten li.: Johanna Elizabeth Christina Fourie, 3. v. oben: ranplett; S. 78 2. v. oben li.: Mike Liu);
Photolibrary, London (S. 63 oben li.: Jack Hollingsworth (RF); S. 78 oben Mitte: Imagebroker.net / Alf Jonsson);
Picture Desk, London (S. 14: THE KOBAL COLLECTION / UNIVERSAL PICTURES);
Shutterstock, New York (S. 11 oben: Piotr Marcinski, unten: Monkey Business Images; S. 63 unten Mitte: Stephen Coburn, unten re.: BlueOrange Studio; S. 65 unten 2. v. li.: Anke van Wyk, unten Mitte: Hedrus, unten re.: Karel Gallas, unten 2. v. re.: EcoPrint; S. 78 oben re.: Simon Krzic, 2. v. unten re.: Kapu, oben li.: Karen Kaspar; S. 80 oben li.: Sashkin, oben Mitte: Sandra Kemppainen, oben re.: Tatiana Popova, Mitte li.: gjfoto, Mitte: BonD80, Mitte re.: Jessmine, unten li.: oksana2010, unten Mitte: sav-in, unten re.: Tatuasha);
ullstein bild, Berlin (S. 13: SIPA)

Textquellen

S. 16 *Tears of a clown* Excerpt from THE ABSOLUTELY TRUE DIARY OF A PART-TIME INDIAN by Sherman Alexie. Copyright © 2007 by Sherman Alexie. By permission of Little, Brown and Company;
S. 30 *Welcome to a year without garbage.* From www.greengarbageproject.com by Amy Korst;
S. 33 *Teenagers and technology.* Abridged from “Teenagers and technology: ‘I’d rather give up my kidney than my phone’” by Jon Henley (http://www.guardian.co.uk/lifeandstyle/2010/jul/16/teenagers-mobiles-facebook-social-networking) © Guardian News & Media Ltd 2010;
S. 47 *Award for teenager who nursed her dying friend* by Genevieve Roberts published in Evening Standard, Monday 28 June 2010;
S. 49 *About the UK Youth Parliament.* Abridged from http://www.ukyouthparliament.org.uk/downloads/UKYP_Manifesto.pdf by kind permission Democracy for Young People (UK Youth Parliament);
S. 51 *Jane Goodall’s Roots & Shoots.* Excerpts from http://www.rootsandshoots.org by kind permission of the Jane Goodall Institute;
S. 67 *The Curious Incident of the Dog in the Night-Time.* Excerpt from “The Curious Incident of the Dog in the Night-Time” by Mark Haddon. © Mark Haddon, 2003. Reprinted by permission of Aitken Alexander Associates Ltd, London;
S. 70 *Das filmende Klassenzimmer.* Adapted from http://www.filmstadt.de/fileadmin/bav_filmstadt/downloads/PDF_KLAZI_09.pdf © Bavaria Filmstadt 2011